HOPE

— for the — Brokenhearted

*God's Voice
of Comfort
in the Midst
of Grief
and Loss*

DR. JOHN LUKE TERVEEN

Victor®

The Bible Teacher's Teacher

COOK COMMUNICATIONS MINISTRIES
Colorado Springs, Colorado • Paris, Ontario
KINGSWAY COMMUNICATIONS LTD
Eastbourne, England

Victor® is an imprint of
Cook Communications Ministries, Colorado Springs, CO 80918
Cook Communications, Paris, Ontario
Kingsway Communications, Eastbourne, England

HOPE FOR THE BROKENHEARTED
© 2006 by John Luke Terveen

Published in association with the literary agency of Sanford Communications, Inc, 6406 NE Pacific St. Portland, OR 97213.

The Web addresses (URLs) recommended throughout this book are solely offered as a resource to the reader. The citation of these Web sites does not in any way imply an endorsement on the part of the author or the publisher, nor does the author or publisher vouch for their content for the life of this book.

Cover Design: Greg Jackson, Thinkpen Design, llc
Cover Photo Credit: ©2006 iStockPhoto

First Printing, 2006
Printed in the United States of America

1 2 3 4 5 6 7 8 9 10 Printing/Year 11 10 09 08 07 06

ISBN-13: 978-0-7814-4362-3
ISBN-10: 0-7814-4362-8

LCCN: 2006924060

Hope for the Brokenhearted

It's emotional. It's theological. It's careful. And it's real—because grief is real. John Terveen takes us through his personal journey from a seminary professor who teaches biblical language to a dad who understands the language of the Father's heart. Here is the strengthening comfort God intended from his Word.

—STU WEBER
PASTOR, GOOD SHEPHERD COMMUNITY CHURCH,
PROMISE KEEPERS SPEAKER, AND AUTHOR OF *TENDER WARRIOR*

Speaking from the personal pain of the death of his daughter, John Terveen delivers an intimate and insightful reflection on grief. Thoroughly biblical yet thoughtfully reflective, the author integrates the emotion of his tragedy with the hope imbedded in Scripture. In this readable book, each chapter, like a well-honed homily, draws from a biblical sage, prophet, or apostle, providing comfort and hope. Oft-forgotten lessons from Asaph, Jeremiah, David, and Paul come alive in this clear and compassionate narrative, and the chapters of Jesus on the Sea of Galilee, in Gethsemane, and on the Emmaus road are like walks with an old friend. So let this quiet gem challenge you to think, summon you to pray, and call you to worship a good God whose goodness may sometimes seem cloaked in sorrow.

—DR. DAN LOCKWOOD
PRESIDENT OF MULTNOMAH BIBLE COLLEGE AND MULTNOMAH BIBLICAL SEMINARY

With realism and keen insight born out of the depths of grief, John Terveen reveals the hope that only God can bring to those who are suffering. I have read many books on grief but none so biblically centered. As you read this book with your Bible open, the Holy Spirit will give you the courage to face your tragedy and the power to walk in God's hope.

—DALE EBEL
SENIOR PASTOR, ROLLING HILLS COMMUNITY CHURCH

Dr. John Terveen rightly reminds us of the inevitability of emotional pain and loss in this life and does so with the clarity of his own grief over the death of his daughter. With a careful analysis of similarly poignant moments in the lives of God's servants, he brilliantly reviews the promises of Scripture and the compassionate character of the God they describe. To those believers struggling with their grief, Dr. Terveen's book is a clarion call to the reality that they are not alone, nor are they without a blueprint for recovery.

—GARY H. LOVEJOY, PhD
PROFESSOR EMERITUS IN PSYCHOLOGY, PRACTICING LICENSED PSYCHOTHERAPIST,
AND RECOGNIZED AUTHORITY ON DEPRESSION

A voice calls down in these chapters, "I, the Almighty One, the King of Love, am your hope. I will carry you through to a sure future." What an opening of truths that lie below the surface of familiar Bible passages! What a solid rock for our slipping feet; what strengthening for each stage of grief.

—PAMELA REEVE
PROFESSOR, MULTNOMAH BIBLICAL SEMINARY,
AUTHOR OF *DESERTS OF THE HEART*

Every writer ought to ask himself before putting words to paper, "Does the world need this book?" In this case, Dr. Terveen should have heard a resounding yes. His gift to us has been costly. But we desperately need his reflections on the pain he suffered when he lost his beloved teen daughter. We equally need the application of all he has learned in his studies and teaching of biblical languages and text regarding death and the hope of resurrection. None of us is exempt from the "valley of the shadow of death," but we can be gifted with what God has told us regarding our last and worst enemy, death, and the sure and certain hope of heaven. How blessed we are to have such a heartfelt resource in our hands!

—PAT PALAU
AUTHOR, SPEAKER, AND WIFE OF EVANGELIST LUIS PALAU

When the Terveens lost Rachel, their little lamb, despair drove them to God's Word. The Scripture drove them into the arms of the God of all comfort. I wish this book had been here when I lost my mother and younger sister. Through Scripture, Terveen reveals that the Lamb who suffered is the safe refuge for all of us who have lost one of our lambs.

—GARRY FRIESEN
AUTHOR OF *DECISION MAKING AND THE WILL OF GOD*

It's refreshing to me to have a critical resource like this that deals with grief in an insightful, biblical manner. Having known Rachel personally and having seen her love for Christ and the impact of her passing, I know this book captures Rachel's ongoing ministry in the lives of others. I would encourage every pastor who ministers to families who have lost a loved one ... to use this book. I appreciate John Terveen's willingness to share this gift with our community of churches.

—STEVE KEELS
GENERAL EDITOR AND AUTHOR OF *TRUTHQUEST* AND
YOUTH PASTOR, GOOD SHEPHERD COMMUNITY CHURCH

Dedicated to

Rachel Louise Terveen
(1985–1999)
My beloved daughter, my little lamb ...

*He gathers the lambs in his arms
and carries them close to his heart.*
—Isaiah 40:11

CONTENTS

ACKNOWLEDGMENTS

When our daughter Rachel died, we were devastated. Yet, in the following months, while we waded through clouds of grief, God gradually and graciously reached into our broken hearts, especially through his Word in Scripture. Hearing the Lord speak through the Bible, we rediscovered hope. Those messages of hope inspired this book and are the essential foundation stones upon which it is built. To God be the glory for his Word.

I especially acknowledge my wife, Laura, for supporting and encouraging me in this difficult work. It's a tender topic. In the process of writing this book, I found myself forced to visit again and again the grief and loss I felt so keenly. Laura's simple presence as a soul mate and fellow sufferer served often to salve my reopened wounds. I also appreciate her admirable service as a regular sounding board for every part of the book, listening in to the various stages of the work as it progressed and offering useful advice where necessary. As we have journeyed this path toward rediscovering hope so intimately together, the book feels in many ways as much Laura's as mine.

I am thankful for the help and support of Marian O'Connor, whose loving encouragement and genuine interest in this writing project over the years always proved timely. I am also grateful to Mr. David Sanford for his belief in this book, his expertise in helping such a project come to fruition, and his relentlessly encouraging spirit. Finally, I wish to thank the faculty and students of Multnomah Biblical Seminary for their supportive and gracious spirit toward me as I have walked through my valley of the shadow of death.

FOREWORD

I remember like it was yesterday hearing the stunning news of the death of fourteen-year-old Rachel Terveen.

Rachel's family was part of our church. Her brother, Matt, was the same age as our daughter Angie. The church and community mourned. Though I didn't know her personally, Rachel has come to my mind often over the years. When I wrote my book *Heaven*, I included her in the dedication.

Rachel was an athlete, young and vibrant … if any death was unthinkable, hers was. Nanci and I looked at our own daughters and realized no one is immune to death. In Psalm 90:12, Moses prayed, "Teach us to number our days aright, that we may gain a heart of wisdom." John Terveen, Rachel's father, has written a book that offers such wisdom.

Hope for the Brokenhearted is honest. It comes from the heart, where at times pain and faith and doubt have slugged it out inside the author. Grief is a journey, often confusing and sometimes terribly lonely. This book isn't full of easy answers—which is good, since there are none. But it *is* full of hope and Christ-centered perspective.

A former pastor, Dr. Terveen is a Greek professor at Multnomah Biblical Seminary, a school I had the privilege of graduating from thirty years ago. His book is steeped in Scripture. It therefore has a power most books don't. Those grieving *need to hear from God*. He promises *his* Word, not ours, will not return to him empty, without accomplishing the purpose for which he sent it (see Isa. 55:11).

Our churches and communities, our nation and our world, are filled with grieving people—numb, broken, bitter, or simply exhausted. They need to hear from someone who has been where they are. John Terveen has been there.

Who of us has not been touched by death? A dear friend of mine died at age nineteen in a terrible farm accident. My uncle was murdered. My mother was suddenly taken by cancer twenty-four years ago. Eleven years later, to the day, I was holding the hand of my closest friend when he died at age thirty-eight. My wife and daughters and brother and I were with my father when he died eight years ago. My wife's dear mother died, and her father is failing this moment. Three families we know have lost one of their beloved parents in the last four weeks. Two days ago a pastor friend conducted the memorial service for his infant granddaughter. On and on it goes. Your list is as long as mine. But here is the good news, and it is breathtaking: One day God "will swallow up death forever" (Isa. 25:8). All that is wrong will be made right. "No longer will there be any curse" (Rev. 22:3).

Jesus said, "Blessed are you who weep now, for you will laugh.... Rejoice in that day and leap for joy, because great is your reward in heaven" (Luke 6:21–23). This is the promise of God: His children who weep now at all their losses will *laugh* in heaven.

I began by saying I didn't know Rachel Terveen personally. That's true, but one day I will meet her. I'll get to hear her laugh. I'll watch the smiles of her father and mother and her Lord Jesus as they look at her. As resurrected people, we'll walk together on God's new earth.

Our Lord promises, "He will wipe away every tear from their eyes;

and there will no longer be any death; there will no longer be any mourning, or crying, or pain" (Rev. 21:4 NASB).

That day may seem distant, but *it is coming*. Bank on it. Until it arrives, I pray that this book will offer you help and assistance on the journey.

—Randy Alcorn

PREFACE

During the difficult times following the death of my teenage daughter, Rachel, my wife and I received support and love from many caring people. We appreciated the kindness of several who—concerned and wanting to help us through our grief—gave us books. We read some and perused others, yet nothing compared to the hope, wisdom, comfort, and strength we discovered in the Bible itself. Through our hearing, reading, and studying God's Word, the Holy Spirit spoke powerfully into our souls, bringing real encouragement and hope to our broken hearts.

So why write this book? Though there are many books on grief and loss issues, few devote themselves to exploring the text of the Bible beyond a single verse or short passage, a style typical of brief devotional books. For many books that address grief and loss, the Bible is a source of illustrations and in the background but not the determining source for their content. Books grounded mostly in counseling principles have their place—as do books of art and poetry, and one-topic biblical thematic studies, and books that journal someone's path through the pain of grief. Yet nothing compares to the Holy Spirit's power in speaking to our hearts through direct, full, and sustained interaction with God's Word.

This book aims to help you take steps down the biblical road toward hope. I will provide a deeper and longer look at special biblical passages that have ministered hope to my own soul. I will occasionally share my own heartbreaking experience, though always keeping the biblical text at the center. The broad theme of "hope for the brokenhearted" forms the backdrop for each chapter, though with careful attention not to abuse the biblical author's purposes in the text. Each chapter ends with a summary of the passage's response to the question: "Where is the hope?" A "Here is my heart, Lord" prayer section follows each chapter, hopefully offering a helpful guide for praying through the text.

Each chapter of this book stands alone; therefore, the chapters may be read in any order. The book's chapter order is canonical, with four chapters each in of three sections: Old Testament, Gospels, and Pauline Epistles. The sections also may be taken in any order. Readers should also consider these simple directions: *First*, pray that God will speak to your heart through his Word. Ask him to help you listen carefully for what he wants to say—not necessarily what you want to hear. *Second*, read the Scripture for the chapter. I have used the New International Version as my main translation, though I occasionally refer to other versions. *Third*, while reading through the chapter, have your Bible open to the passage so that you can consult it regularly. Hang in there with some of the more difficult passages such as 1 Corinthians 15. *Finally*, be sure to follow up your reading with prayer. To help, I have provided a guide to help you pray through the Scripture after each chapter. My prayer is that the Lord will minister his comfort and hope to your heart through his Word, as he has done to mine.

THE LAST HURDLE … AND HOPE

In April 1999, our fourteen-year-old daughter, Rachel, suffered a fatal heart attack during a late-afternoon track practice at her middle school. A champion high hurdler, Rachel had soared over her last hurdle and, like a lamb, leaped straight into the arms of the Good Shepherd, Jesus. Her fight now finished, her race now run, her faith firmly held to the end, Rachel departed to be with her Lord Jesus.

The media covered her death extensively, and thousands came to her funeral service—a tribute to her loving spirit. In the wake of her life and death, many put their faith in Christ. In this we rejoice. We, however, remain here—awaiting with deep longing our reunion with her again in heaven. In a very real way our grief and agonizing sense of loss will never end this side of glory, so for now we live on in hope—a hope God graciously has spoken into our souls most clearly through his Word in Scripture. It is my great desire that sharing my encounter with the God of all comfort through these scriptural passages will bring healing and hope to fellow travelers on the pathway of grief and loss.

[I presented the following comments for Rachel's memorial service at Good Shepherd Community Church. They serve well as a necessary and fitting personal prelude for the reader to the interactions with God's Word that follow.]

Before she was born, we could imagine no other name for her than Rachel, "little lamb." It fit her perfectly. Soft, pure, gentle, playful, and a joy bringer to all who touched her and were touched by her. Our family calendar was full of her activities and plans, a calendar looked at now only with a sense of pain and profound loss. The emptiness in our hearts from her absence is almost unbearable at times.

We well remember her birth. It also made news headlines in Sioux Falls, South Dakota: "Newborn Didn't Want to Sit Out the Storm." The night before her birth we had a classic spring South Dakota snowstorm. Her mother woke up in the wee hours of the morning and said it was time. Well-meaning Dad fired up the car only to get it stuck in the wet snow that clogged the streets. Time to call 911. Shortly after, down our street came a snowplow, followed by a police car, followed by an ambulance. What a parade ride to the hospital! Rachel was always ready to live life to the fullest—and she wanted to get started, snowstorm or not.

Some tenderhearted memories include her love for animals. She loved cats and dogs both, but cats especially. Her massive yellow tabby cat, Max, let her hold him like a big baby and would tenderly put his paw on her cheek while she lovingly held him. We often remarked how he allowed no one else to do that but her. We thought it was his way of saying to her: "Rachel, you are precious to me." And so she was— wonderfully precious to us all.

Another animal she treasured was her older brother, Matthew. In fact, as an eight-year-old in school, she wrote a humorous short story about him titled "My Brother Is a Pain." It reads simply, "My brother is a pain. My brother bugs me all the time. In the car he always tells on me, but he really does what he says [I do]. I really, really wish I was the oldest. When my brother leaves forever I can watch what I want on TV. Always my brother gets to stay up. My mom says I'm too little to stay up. When he goes to a friend's house to spend the night it is very nice, but it gets kind of lonely. Sometime he takes trolls away. I always tell my mom. I think my brother is a pain. My brother is the oldest child. His name is Matthew. Matthew is thirteen. He is a rude child. When my mom and dad say I can have ice cream he eats it all." Pretty typical of brother-and-sister relations—teasing and yet loving. He was quietly proud of her and her accomplishments and anticipated supporting her and cheering her on as she grew up. They simply loved each other.

Matthew and Rachel often kidded us about being like the mythical Chevy Chase family, the Griswolds, on vacation. Station wagon, dog, doofus dad, funny mom, brother, and sister—all the ingredients for big fun. Our life was full of goofy and joyful adventures as we took our vacations together across the United States. Rich, rich memories.

I remember Rachel's many friends. They were of all types. She did not turn away from anyone. They were often at our house. Eighty to ninety percent of the calls to our house began, "Is Rachel there?" It had become harder and harder to get through on the phone to our house. The calls came from an incredibly diverse group of people. Her trademark was her kindness to everyone. Friends from her school—teachers, parents, classmates. Friends from volleyball teams at school and a club—coaches, teammates, and parents. They all remember her jumping so high and spiking so hard. On the track they remember her running so gracefully as she soared easily over the hurdles. So many first places. So much fun. Friends from music and band—and the joyfully played flute.

We dearly remember all the little things. A wake-up knock in early morning. A good-night hug and "I love you." A walk together with her dog Whiskers. A sled ride down an icy street, stacked on top of each other, laughing all the way down. A long bike ride through the country-side together. A ride to school. "Love you; have a good day." A thousand little ways Rachel was the center of our lives. We will miss her deeply, in a thousand little, yet large, ways.

I remember how Rachel loved *The Wizard of Oz*. You know the story line. Dorothy is caught away in a windy maelstrom far from her home in Kansas to the strange land of Oz. Judy Garland beautifully sings the theme song, a song Rachel and I sang from memory as we drove around together in the car.

> Somewhere over the rainbow, way up high; there's a land that I've heard of, once in a lullaby. Somewhere over the rainbow, skies are blue; and the dreams that you dare to dream really do come true. Someday I'll wish upon a star, and wake up where the clouds are far behind me; where troubles melt like lemon drops away above the chimney tops, that's where you'll find me. Somewhere over the rainbow, bluebirds fly; birds fly over the rainbow, why, oh, why can't I? (from the motion picture *The Wizard of Oz*, MGM Studios, 1939, directed by Victor Fleming; music by Harold Arlen and lyrics by E. Y. Harburg)

Dorothy's song was a beautiful but sad song about the desire to "go home." Rachel has gone home, not to Kansas, but to her eternal home in heaven to be with the Lord Jesus, safe forever in his arms.

We remember when our little lamb Rachel gave her life to Jesus Christ as her Savior and Lord. She was seven years old and prayed a childlike prayer with her mother. It was a joy to see her faith develop and mature as she began to live more and more like her Master, Jesus.

Rachel loved nothing more than reaching out to other people, even as Jesus reached out and gave himself to her and us all. You could give no greater gift in memory of Rachel than to give your own life to her God, wholeheartedly and truly. If you put your heart in Jesus' hands, accept him as your own Savior who forgives all your sins, and know him as your Lord who will unerringly lead you to heaven, it will be a piece of grace in the midst of grief.

Though we always knew it deep in our hearts, we have come to a crystal clear awareness of the truth that the only thing in this world that matters is love—a love embodied perfectly in Jesus our Lord. So until we meet again, we cry out from our hearts, "Rachel, our little lamb, we love you from here to the moon and back again."

He gathers the lambs in his arms and
carries them close to his heart.
—ISAIAH 40:11

Part One

VISIONS OF HOPE

Chapter 1

WILL FAITH SURVIVE?

 Psalm 73

*When a crisis of faith edges you near
the brink of despair and unbelief, enter
again into God's sanctuary to worship,
and there embrace anew both God himself
and his true eternal perspectives on life.*

In the sorrowful season following the loss of Rachel, in the spring of 1999, I experienced a real crisis of faith. I found attending church to be especially difficult, as bouncy praise choruses seemed to fall flat and even felt false. The simple little chorus "God is so good. God is so good. God is so good. He's so good to me" presented a special struggle for me. How in the world could a *good* God allow such a loving, believing, and pure-hearted girl to die? What's "good" about that? "God is so good. He's so good to me"? Honestly, sometimes I almost choked on the words. And so my struggle of faith would go, driving me to the cliff edge of despair and even unbelief.

Nevertheless, my wife and I continued to go to church and enter into worship. Where else would we go? Over time, as again and again we came to worship in God's house, we sensed that we had come into his very presence. We entered to worship—usually weakly, sometimes awkwardly, and frequently tearfully. Yet in the community of his people we experienced the Scriptures read, the songs sung, the sermons shared ... and bit by bit, through these humble acts of worship, I encountered God's real presence with me again, and I embraced anew both God himself and eternal realities about the life of faith here and life hereafter. Hope was reawakened. Though such a struggle has ebbed and flowed, at that time I experienced a real turning point in the renewal of my faith and a reawakened hope for the future.

WHEN A CRISIS OF FAITH EDGES YOU NEAR THE BRINK OF DESPAIR AND UNBELIEF, *ENTER* AGAIN INTO GOD'S SANCTUARY TO WORSHIP AND THERE *EMBRACE* ANEW BOTH HIM AND TRUE ETERNAL LIFE PERSPECTIVES.

What an encouragement, then, to discover in Psalm 73 a fellow struggler—Asaph (composer of twelve psalms and a worship choir leader), who also wrestled mightily with this issue. Here in a psalm/song, Asaph exhibits a mature fruit of the faith life, born out of his honest struggles. Through Psalm 73, God's Word calls out to us: *When a crisis of faith edges you near the brink of despair and unbelief,* enter *again into God's sanctuary to worship and there* embrace *anew both him and true eternal life perspectives.*

EDGING NEAR THE CLIFF OF DESPAIR AND UNBELIEF (PS. 73:1–16)

The first sixteen verses of Psalm 73 reveal a basic problem that drives Asaph crazily careening toward the cliff edge of despair and unbelief: Why do good people suffer while bad people seem to prosper? This issue has befuddled generations of deep thinkers. Yet this presents no mere intellectual dilemma or theological puzzle for Asaph but is a matter of life and death—a deadly serious question of the survival of faith itself. Psalm 73 gives his honest confession, a window into the soul of an ordinary man struggling for a real communion of faith with his God. Will faith survive? It is no idle question, neither for him nor for us.

Foundation and Foothold

Almost curiously, Asaph begins with his positive confession that God surely is good (v. 1), though it becomes immediately apparent that he has not always been so sure of that conclusion, nor is it one to which he came easily. He clings to this foundational truth, almost anxiously pushing it up to the front of his song as if he needs to say it out loud before the long and desperately dark thoughts that follow. It is a prime principle, a fine conclusion—but a problematic one, for it begs the question: In a life of woes, what sense does it make to hold on to a belief in a God who is good? Indeed, the force of this question so rattles Asaph's spiritual cage that he poetically says he nearly lost his "foothold," slipped, and fell (v. 2). *Why* he nearly tumbled down now dominates his thoughts in his song.

Asaph looks around at people who totally disrespect God—who are dishonest and even arrogant about it—and sees that life is pretty good for them. They have their health, wealth, the respect of others, and a relatively untroubled existence. When he sees this, it magnifies his own sense of loss in his suffering. He feels deprived and denied of what good people, people "pure in heart" and not bad people, ought to receive. Instead, he sees the bad guys of the world better off than he is, prospering and seemingly immune to the hard knocks they so richly deserve. In his vivid description of this (vv. 3–12), two emotions especially enter his heart—embittered envy and frustrated, simmering anger.

Embittered Envy

Asaph confesses his envious spirit (vv. 3–5). Perhaps nothing blinds us so much as envy and the sense of grievance that often accompanies loss. Deprived of what we perceive as "ours" by all rights, it bothers us to see others who still have those things, those people, or those relationships. We're bitterly reminded not only of our past loss but of our present and future denials as well. The blinding power of envy is then unleashed.

Following the death of our daughter, one of the more difficult things for us was just to see her young teenage friends. We loved them and appreciated their good intentions toward us, but their presence hurt. Even now, years later, when I see one of her friends somewhere—now grown older—I sometimes find myself avoiding them. I envy their health, their joy, and their life. Even more troublesome yet can be a simple trip to the grocery store or to the local mall, only to see a mother and her young teenage daughter walking happily together, shopping, and talking. The loss is magnified and envy creeps in unbidden. That should be us. The list of experiences that create an embittered envy goes on—girls in their lovely prom dresses, a televised high school volleyball tournament, graduation, wedding gowns, and little grandchildren. We should have had that; it should have been ours.

Frustrated Anger

Often closely related to envy, a frustrated anger may also rise up (vv. 6–12). Especially in view of bad people prospering, Asaph indignantly complains that they wear their arrogance like so much jewelry (v. 6); do not hesitate to step on people cruelly to get what they want (vv. 6–8); verbally and physically mistreat others (v. 8); and, worst of all, totally disrespect God (vv. 9–11). With frustration mounting, he grumbles that these foul fat cats seem to have a life of ease and increasing prosperity (v. 12). The bad get blessed while the righteous get ripped off.

It drives Asaph to wonder aloud whether devoting his life to being loyal to God and trusting him—being "pure in heart" (vv. 1, 13)—has been "in vain," just a giant waste of time (vv. 13–14). Is faith in God futile? Wrestling mightily with a grievous loss, C. S. Lewis in *A Grief Observed* rails at length against God on this count, broaching openly the matter of God

HIS FAITH FAMILY BECOMES FOR HIM A NEEDED BRAKE AND EVEN A SORT OF SIGNPOST DIRECTING HIM BACK TO GOD.

knowing what he was doing. Lewis almost loses it, intemperately wondering whether God took some perverse pleasure in the suffering of good people—whether God was a "Cosmic Sadist."[1] Surely God could do better! Lewis's frustrated outpouring of his soul's anguished anger, teetering on the edge of despair and unbelief, shares much in common with Asaph. Their bracing brand of honesty unnerves us, although many of us know that feeling well. It may remain unspoken, and we may feel it unsafe to voice it, but it is there—a simmering, angry frustration. In the morning, Asaph drags himself out of bed, wondering if God is somehow punishing him (v. 14).

This is dealt with in a meaningful way in a television series called *Joan of Arcadia*. The series revolves around high school teenager Joan—a thinly veiled allusion to Joan of Arc—her parents, a wheelchair-bound older brother, and a nerdy genius younger brother. Aside from Joan receiving regular, albeit perplexing, guidance from figures representing God, one major subplot concerns her athletic big-man-on-campus older brother who was crippled in a car accident. At the wheel, drunk, had been his best friend. Of course the drunk driver friend walks away uninjured as so commonly and irritatingly happens in real life. Each character wrestles in a different way with this loss, though the emotions of envy, frustration, anger, guilt, and depression bubble repeatedly to the surface. How they deal with these feelings in the varying contexts of real-life relationships: work, school, family, church—often becomes the insightful heart-hinge upon which the show turns. How like Asaph in Psalm 73, where similar feelings form the *spiritual* heart-hinges upon which his song's message turns.

One such spiritual turning point occurs when Asaph remembers the other members of his family of faith (v. 15). His experience of suffering does not take place in a vacuum but affects others he cares for deeply. In light of this relationship, he pulls back from lashing out publicly with his feelings, sensing that it would have betrayed their communion of faith and love. In a way, his faith family becomes for him a needed brake and even a sort of signpost directing him back to God.

WE MUST CONTINUE TALKING HONESTLY WITH HIM, BUT ALSO—AND THIS IS THE PART WE SOMETIMES FORGET—*LISTENING* CAREFULLY TO WHAT HE DOES CHOOSE TO REVEAL WITH A MIND TO DOING SOMETHING ABOUT IT.

No Answer

Having now fully vented, Asaph feels worn out emotionally and spiritually by his tireless "why" questions. He grimly concludes that all his considerable efforts at figuring this out ended in failure—he still has no answer (v. 16). In fact, he found the effort downright "painful" (KJV) and "oppressive." His deep yearning for an explanation produced nothing, it seems, but an oppressive gloom hanging over him now like a cloud.

In Psalm 73, Asaph sounds a lot like the book of Job—just a simpler and shorter version. It might be called Job-in-a-nutshell. In Job, some "comforters" approached him in the midst of his suffering and offered a variety of answers to his painful "why" questions. But Job's comforters brought neither answer nor comfort. Even today such comforters may come—seemingly more with their agenda than ours—and all too often leave behind equally dismal results.

Some might say it was fruitless or even wrong for Asaph—or us—to go down this impassioned path of anguished questioning. "Don't ask why," they counsel. "Don't even go there," they warn. But Asaph does "go there" and without abandoning his faith. His doubts do not lead to unbelief. Only real faith could be troubled by such things. Is it okay to ask such questions? Yes, so long as we do not descend into endless self-pity; despise God as evil; or cut ourselves off from meaningful, healing relationships. It is critical, however, to continue the conversation with God as a true dialogue. We must continue talking honestly with him, but also—and this is the part we sometimes forget—*listening* carefully to what he does choose to reveal with a mind to doing something about it. Yet it seems Asaph first had to fail in order to understand, for only in declaring the reflections of his human mind a failure do his eyes begin to look beyond himself and what they now see for resolution. Only then does he perceive anew a pathway through his pain and back toward hope.

ENTER AGAIN INTO THE SANCTUARY OF GOD (PS. 73:17)

Turning Point

That cloud of frustrated and oppressive unknowing would have remained hanging over Asaph's head had he not "entered the sanctuary of God" (v. 17). This single line of the psalm dramatically marks the turning point of Asaph's spiritual journey with the little word *till*. When he enters again into God's sanctuary, his path takes on a new direction.

IN SUCH A TIME SIMPLY *ENTERING* CONSTITUTES A MOMENTOUS ACT OF TRUST AND HOPE — A CRITICAL CROSSROADS AT THE BEGINNING OF THE PROCESS OF REDISCOVERING HOPE.

Interestingly, Asaph was probably involved in leadership of the choir music for the Jerusalem tabernacle/temple. (He may have lived to see Solomon's temple built.) Attending "church" was familiar ground for him. In the midst of a crisis of faith, however, such familiar ground may be awkward and painful because of its very familiarity—and therefore all the more tempting to avoid. I vividly remember, after my mother's sudden and unexpected death, my father sitting in church that next Sunday, painfully and tearfully alone despite his children nearby. Going to church was no easy decision that Lord's Day, since he anticipated how just being there would sharpen his sense of loss. Yet he went, sobbing in his seat, feeling bereft of his beloved wife and friend of over forty years. Little did I expect to undergo a similar feeling when my daughter died. Just going to church, where mere days before she had sat next to us and sung the songs of faith, so sharpened our sense of loss and emptiness that we felt tempted to avoid entering into the sanctuary of God. Yet we, too, entered again, feeling bankrupt, broken, and desperate. I discovered that just being there was an act of faith. In such a time simply *entering* constitutes a momentous act of trust and hope—a critical crossroads at the beginning of the process of rediscovering hope.

Taking Time to Worship

Now Asaph knows that he does not enter the sanctuary of God to just sit, but with determined purpose—to worship. The "sanctuary" was well understood to be the place where God's own presence dwelt in a real way and where his people would gather to ascribe glory and honor to him as well as to listen for his Word to them. So there Asaph encounters the living God, together in communion with God's people, through sharing in humble acts of worship. However

WORSHIP CONSISTS NOT MERELY IN THE ACTS WE PERFORM OR THE WORDS WE SPEAK, BUT ALSO IN THE HUMBLE AND TRUSTING LISTENING FOR THE VOICE OF GOD.

weakly, doubtfully, awkwardly, or tearfully, still he comes, trusting that there he will meet his God. Worship consists not merely in the acts we perform or the words we speak, but also in the humble and trusting listening for the voice of God. For, in that submitted listening, we hear anew what an all-wise and all-loving God *does* desire to reveal to us. It may not be our questions or the answers we would like—he does remain sovereign—but learning in God's presence what he does reveal holds the key to the rediscovery of hope and the survival of faith itself.

Embrace Anew True Eternal Perspectives on Life (Ps. 73:18–28)

In worship, God helps Asaph peer beyond the mere here and now and reveals the final destiny of both those who have little or no place for God in their lives and those who do. Asaph embraces anew God's true eternal perspectives on life, and so, too, must we embrace them anew. In the remainder of his psalm, Asaph explores the stark contrast between the destinies of those distant from God and those drawn near to him.

Dismissed and Distant

Asaph now perceives, through God's eyes, the terrible end ahead for those who are "unfaithful to you" (v. 27). From God's point of view, those who have distanced themselves from him are *not* standing on solid ground but on a slippery surface. They are *not* strong and secure, but swept away and destroyed. They are *not* real and lasting, for God despises and dismisses such superficial, outward apparent successes like so many bad dreams that go poof in the real light of morning. Such a sobering eternal perspective should cause us to reevaluate an envious and angry spirit toward the unfaithful. Rather, in light of such an eternal perspective, how we should pity those who blindly and recklessly pursue such a path of emptiness, illusion, and destruction.

Asaph understands further the personal nature of such divine judgment, for he describes them as "those who are *far from you*" (v. 27). In the last analysis, judgment is God's personal rejection, his dismissal of someone as of no further consequence. Jesus concisely sums up what God says on that day in the appalling words: "I never knew you. Away from me, you evildoers" (Matt. 7:23). In "The Weight of Glory," a famous sermon of C. S. Lewis, he captures this horrific reality: "We can be left utterly and absolutely *outside*—repelled, exiled, estranged, finally and unspeakably ignored."[2] What an appalling end, to be dismissed and distanced from God personally and irrevocably.

In retrospect, and in light of this terrible end, Asaph repents honestly of his earlier embittered attitude, recognizing it as mere animal-like instinct and ignorance of God's eternal perspectives (vv. 19–20). Grieving apart from entering again into God's sanctuary and embracing anew his true eternal perspectives about life would have short-circuited Asaph's rediscovery of hope.

Drawn Near into Intimacy

On the other hand, Asaph confesses, "It is good to be *near* God" (v. 28). In stark contrast with being dismissed and distant, when we hold on to faith in God, we find ourselves drawn closer to him in intimacy. Not accidentally, in the New Testament believers learn to address God as "Abba, Father," a family term that pictures God hugging believers on his lap. It is a place of intimate, warm relationship and love—of being "noticed" (Lewis's term in that same sermon) and not ignored. As Lewis further preached, "We can be called in, welcomed, received, acknowledged."[3] Asaph unpacks this wonderful relationship along two key lines—what God *does* for us and what God *is* for us.

Grasped, Guided, Glorified

Asaph voices the momentous "yet" of real faith (v. 23), knowing anew that despite appearances, he had never really been abandoned. God was there all along. Although sometimes our grip slips, God's *grasp* is fast— "you hold me by my right hand" (v. 23). Though we may sometimes feel rudderless in life, he *guides* us with his counsel, his Word always leading us in wisdom and love. And at the climax of it all, he *glorifies* us, and we receive the crowning joy of passing into his presence fully and finally. Oh, how Asaph's concern for the "pure in heart" here in Psalm 73 resonated with the later words of Jesus: "Blessed are the pure in heart, for *they will see God"* (Matt. 5:8). C. S. Lewis spoke of humankind's innate, lifelong yearning to be fully in union with God as finally realized in glory: "To be at last summoned inside would be both glory and honour beyond all our merits and also the healing of that old ache."[4] Those who have suffered and experienced great loss know that "old ache" well—the longing to see God, to be sure, but also longing for the realization of that joyous prospect of seeing again loved ones who have preceded us into glory. Paul, too, understood well that our lives now lead toward this hidden glory: "I consider that our present sufferings are not worth comparing with the glory that will be revealed in us" (Rom. 8:18). The "old ache," you see, will one day be utterly and gloriously relieved, and it will hurt no more.

Sufficiency, Strength, Shelter

Asaph concludes by recalling also what God *is* for him, beginning by affirming God's total *sufficiency* for his life even now—he is all Asaph needs or desires (v. 25)! My mother's childhood Bible is an old Gothic-print German edition of Luther's translation that reads bluntly and to the point: "As long as I have thee, I wish for nothing else in heaven or on earth" (*Wenn ich nur dich habe, so frage ich nichts nach Himmel und Erde*). Suffering is not abolished. It continues, but it is victoriously endured in faith communion with God. Paul's infamous "thorn in the flesh" (likely some nasty physical ailment) caused him suffering, yet God would not intervene to remove it. Paul, however, enduring through faith, recognized afresh that God's grace is sufficient. He would not only cope spiritually but also prosper through the sufficiency of Christ.

Even if life unravels and death itself is faced—"my flesh and my heart may fail" (v. 26)—God remains for Asaph the "*strength* [literally 'rock'] of my heart" and an indestructible purpose ("my portion forever") for living. God is our strength and support until the end of our days. Suffering may well continue, but in its own peculiar way, living by faith in God through suffering embodies a piece of eternity breaking into our broken world. Finally, Asaph calls God his "refuge," a *shelter* to which he can flee when the rains of suffering beat against him. Ira Sankey, a songwriter and musical leader like Asaph, captures this beautifully in his hymn: "The Lord's our Rock; in Him we hide, a shelter in the time of storm. Secure whatever ill betide, a shelter in the time of storm. O Jesus is a rock in a weary land ... a shelter in the time of storm."

Where Is the Hope?

When I was a seminary student, my theology professor, a brilliant, beloved, and passionate man of God, would often almost comically lean over the lectern on his tiptoes and tell us breathlessly from the depth of his heart that this or that teaching about God was "great stuff." And so it was. But what made me really believe him were my weekly tours for clinical pastoral education in a nearby hospital's oncology wing—where my dear professor's wife was steadily losing her battle with cancer. Week by week he would tutor us in the wonders of God. Week by week she would lose a few more pounds, until at last it seemed she would be pure spirit. She weighed a mere sixty pounds or so when her body finally succumbed and she died.

I will never forget her funeral where my dear professor sat brokenhearted but tearfully singing a song of profoundest faith—a paraphrase of Psalm 23: "The King of love my shepherd is, whose goodness faileth never. I nothing lack if I am his and he is mine forever.... And so through all the length of days, thy goodness faileth never. Good Shepherd, may I sing thy praise within thy house forever." There is the hope in a goodness that never fails but grasps us firmly and forever no matter the circumstances. There is the hope in a sufficiency found in him who is forever our Good Shepherd and who guides us now by his wise counsel. There is the hope in a communion with the Lord that begins even now and will be consummated one day when we all, as his children, join him together in glory indescribable.

"Here Is My Heart, Lord ..."

There are times, God, when some things happen that make me wonder about your goodness and really make me struggle with my faith in you, such as when ...

Lord, my suffering/loss makes me feel as if I've lost something really valuable to me, something that should have been mine to enjoy. I admit I feel envious of others, and when I see them, I feel terribly deprived of ...

Sometimes my anger, God, almost overwhelms me with frustration when I see ...

Although I don't feel much like "entering your sanctuary," Lord, because it hurts and the pain seems so hard to face again, yet ...

God, when I worship with your people, help me during the songs, the Scriptures being read, and the sermon being shared once again to ...

When I think, Lord, of the worldly successes and joys of some people who have no real place for you in their lives, help me to remember that ...

When I don't sense you being near to me, I want to recall in faith and reaffirm with thanksgiving what you are doing and will do for me ...

... And also who you are for me now and forevermore ...

Lord, your Word in Psalm 73 ends, "I will tell of all your deeds." Help me to share what I've learned of you and hope through this psalm by ...

Chapter 2

A DEATH MOST PRECIOUS

 PSALM 116

*Face-to-face with death, the psalmist survives
to tell his story in song, an honest testimony that
reflects a difficult passage in his journey of faith.
Moved deeply by the knowledge that God considers
his life something precious, he shares the life-changing
insights he has gained. Those insights propel him
onward with hopeful purpose and direction as he
goes on to "walk in the land of the living."*

Some churches set aside times for people to share a "testimony." These opportunities may be structured or left relatively spontaneous. Several months after our daughter died, our wound still raw and open, the church we attended happened to have one of these testimony times. As usual, people were encouraged to stand and share what God was doing in their lives. At the time, and afterward, I noticed that all those who spoke shared wonderful and positive ways in which God had blessed them. We heard stories of health regained, jobs secured, relationships made stronger, and relatives coming to faith. Appropriately, shared joy and "amens" greeted these stories of blessing. But I remember how awkward and out of it I felt when—silenced in the face of such obvious blessings—I felt myself so unblessed. I wondered if anyone else left feeling as spiritually bereft as I did or whether I was as alone as I felt.

WHEN DEEPLY DISTRESSED BY SORROW AND LOSS, DEPEND ON GOD FOR DELIVERANCE AND DISCOVER ANEW HOPEFUL AND PURPOSEFUL DIRECTION.

Is God absent from the valleys of our lives? How typical for people to revel in the "yeses" and "successes" as we recount *answers* to prayer. But what of the struggles, of the "nos" and the "not yets"? Are they not answers, too? Is God not there also, and does he not care? To talk about the "no" or "not yet" experiences of our faith journey creates levels of discomfort. We worry about being a spiritual failure or a downer, so we suppress our hurt and hold on for another time and another place, which too often never come. Sadly, the pain usually comes out anyway, even if sideways, in inappropriate ways and places. It would be wonderfully healthy for the people of God to create space for sharing testimonies that reflect the full range of the journey of faith—the many stations of trust visited on the tracks of life's trials, hard decisions, disappointments, and heartaches. Interestingly, in Psalm 116:10 the writer challenges us with seemingly paradoxical words to a fuller and more real, if uncomfortable, authenticity: "I believed; therefore I said, 'I am greatly afflicted.'" Suffering, yes, but in the context of a testimony of faith.

Music communicates the diversity of human experience. My own tastes are eclectic, running from Eric Clapton to Gustav Mahler's *Resurrection Symphony*, from stately hymns of faith to contemporary choruses, and from Randy Travis to cellist Yo-Yo Ma playing the hauntingly beautiful movie theme of *The Mission*. As the great musical songbook of the Bible, the Psalms lyrically express a broad spiritual spectrum of human emotion and experience. Some praise attributes of God's greatness; others give thanks, confess sin and seek forgiveness, pour out pain and heartbreak, vent anger, mourn loss, rejoice on a special occasion (royal coronation), and testify to God's delivering power. The Psalms, like life itself, are not monochrome but musically paint a richly diverse, complex, and multilayered picture of the believer's experiences and the human story. Truly, they are psalms for all seasons and the souls of all saints, meant to be sung together and shared in the community choir of faith singers.

The setting of Psalm 116 is a testimony, the personal sharing of an intensely meaningful part of the psalmist's experience—a spiritual slice of life from his life story. We could call Psalm 116 a *survivor psalm*, a song of heartfelt love and thanks to God composed after barely surviving a life-threatening illness. As a testimony, his song reveals crucial spiritual keynotes that still today give us vital lessons for surviving in and walking through the valley of the shadow of death. Though Psalm 116 celebrates its author's survival, the vivid memory of that brush with death throws into sharp relief these important spiritual survivalist lessons. When deeply distressed by sorrow and loss, depend on God for deliverance and discover anew hopeful and purposeful direction. These truths can redemptively impact the lives not only of those who themselves live on to testify but also of those for whom things turn out differently and who may find themselves left behind wrestling with the reality of grievous loss.

DISTRESSED AT DEATH'S DOOR

Dire Straits

Though he gives no specifics, likely the psalmist had experienced some major physical sickness or injury that brought him to death's door (vv. 3, 8, 15). This close call with death sets the context for understanding the power of his testimony. He clearly sensed the nearness of the grave. The deadly seriousness of his situation cast a broad, dark shadow.

He remembers his deep feelings at the time, drawing out through his song's lyrical imagery vivid word pictures of his soul's distress. It felt like cords wrapped around his throat like a noose (v. 3), tightening and holding ever more firmly despite all efforts to escape. One can almost feel his trapped, animal-like panic when, attempting to get away and draw in more breath, he finds he cannot do it. Worn out from the desperate effort, the cords bound him like "chains" (v. 16) and weighed down his spirit. Overcome by his anguish and grief, he lies down feeling "completely crushed" (v. 10 JB) and grimly awaiting the inevitable end.

The bodies we now possess are not built for immortality. They are more fragile than often imagined and susceptible to any number of deadly ailments and injuries that respect neither person nor age. Life-sapping diseases like cancer, diabetes, heart disease, "letter diseases" (ALS, MS, etc.), and many other terrible scourges lay waste to the human body. Despite our tenacious teenager-like denial ("It will never happen to me or to my loved ones"), suffering, grief, loss, and death remain inescapable realities that eventually dot everyone's life landscape. Denial and avoidance only delay the experience but can never deliver us through these valleys. However difficult it may be, honestly expressing our heart's feelings as the psalmist did begins to loosen the chains of a suffocating anguish that chokes and binds us, opening new avenues for healing and hope.

Disillusionment with People

Now, it was bad enough that the psalmist had to struggle with his physical problems, but to top it off he found himself also fighting against people at the same time. "And in my dismay I said, 'All men are liars'" (v. 11). It seems that when it rained on the psalmist, it really poured. He found himself dismayed and disillusioned with people precisely at his weakest time when he could have used a helping hand. Though the specifics of the problem with people are not made clear, his poetic hyperbole clearly expresses his intense feeling that "the help of man is worthless" (Ps. 60:11). He felt utterly let down (or even intentionally hurt) by people and almost bitterly concludes that humans are but an empty hope, hollow and untrustworthy. However extreme the psalmist's sentiment might seem, his bottom line was that, at a primary and fundamental level, fickle and fallible people cannot be relied on.

GOD KEEPS ON LISTENING TO US AND KNOWS FAR MORE OF OUR SITUATION THAN WE IMAGINE.

Decision to Call on the Lord

So at the lowest time, in the midst of his anguish over his terrible situation and dismay with people, right then the psalmist turned to God: "Then I called on the name of the LORD" (v. 4; a phrase repeated in vv. 13, 17). Realizing that he could not rely on human beings, he grasps on to God and cries out to him for mercy and deliverance (vv. 1, 4). But this calling on the name of a merciful and saving God does not come out of nowhere. His relationship of trust and faith in the Lord has provided him grounds for hope and a confidence to talk openly and honestly to God about his pain and heartache: "I believed; therefore I said, 'I am greatly afflicted'" (v. 10). It is just *because* he "believes" that he can voice his anguish and sorrow. Only in light of such a relationship of trust does such personal vulnerability make sense and then bear the fruits of new hope. The old hymn asks: "Where could I go, oh, where could I go? Seeking a shelter from the storm … where could I go but to the Lord?" To the Lord the psalmist went, calling on his name as a merciful and saving God; and so, too, may we all depend upon the Lord and call on his name.

Depend on God for Deliverance

Is God there? Does he really care and pay attention? Sometimes in the midst of grief, the sense of silence and aloneness can almost overwhelm us (v. 3). We cannot see beyond the pain, and we even question things we long thought we believed. To such a broken and conflicted soul Psalm 116 sings out, reminding our hearts of what God is really like—that he is there and that he cares deeply for us. Such a vision of God calls out for our trust. He is worthy of it.

Read My Ears!

Psalm 116 begins with an affirmation of love: "I love the LORD." Such affection arises as a response to God's own love, a divine love that *listens long and well.* The Hebrew verb in verse 1, often translated "[has] heard," actually accents the continuing nature ("he hears") of God's hearing. God keeps on listening to us and knows far more of our situation than we imagine. For the psalmist, God's persistent hearing is a lasting assurance of his loving listening, not a mere reminiscence of an experience in the past. He heard my cry then, continues to hear me now, and surely will hear me in the future too. God is a great and persevering listener, a vital part of his grace to us all.

Several years ago in a presidential election campaign, one candidate emphatically declared, "Read my lips," as he promised firmly never to raise taxes. The little phrase at the time was a punchy and popular way of stressing and clarifying what someone was saying. But sometimes the fact that we listen carefully speaks far more loudly than anything we say. Ears may communicate better than mouths. Here, then, God effectively says to the psalmist, "*Read my ears!*" God listens long and well, a reality that bestows on someone a deep sense of being heard, valued, and respected. "Being heard" is a critically important way station on a spiritual journey through difficult times.

GOD EXPERIENCES ANGUISH TOO AS HE GRIEVES WITH US IN OUR SUFFERING AND LOSS.

The psalmist beautifully captures the caring and loving listening of God with another poetic image: "He hath inclined his ear unto me" (v. 2 KJV). This pictures God bending down and leaning his head toward us to hear us all the better, lovingly accommodating his greatness to our smallness. When I come home from work, I often will greet my three-year-old and five-year-old daughters with a hug and then bend down to their level and hold them close to me so that they can tell me of some important event in their day. By patiently listening at their level, bending down to pay attention to them, I reaffirm our closeness in a joyful and loving father-daughter relationship. God does just that when he turns "his ear to me" (v. 2) to listen to what important events have transpired in my day.

Reaches Out to the Helpless

You see, God especially reaches out his protective hand to help those who cannot help themselves—the "simplehearted" who have been driven to their knees by the hard knocks of life (v. 6). Those whose childlike faith has taught them humility fully recognize their helplessness and turn to God in trust. D. L. Moody once said, "God sends no one away empty except those who are full of themselves."

Jesus' words in Matthew 5:3 have long fascinated me: "Blessed are the poor in spirit, for theirs is the kingdom of heaven." Those Jesus says are "blessed" are precisely those who likely feel least "blessed." And yet, Jesus teaches that those humble "poor in spirit" people are precisely the ones—the psalmist's simplehearted ones—in whom God's protective power is manifested! The emphatically placed word "theirs" in Matthew 5:3 tells us that God's kingdom, his rule in all its life-giving and saving power, belongs to them and consists of them. The "poor in spirit" are blessed just because they know how desperately needy they really are—completely dependent upon the grace of God. Coming to grips with our helplessness is the first and most important requirement for receiving God's gracious help in our own suffering and hurt. Such guileless and childlike trust from the simplehearted remains the indispensable starting point in knowing God's loving hand of protection and care. When brought to our knees, God reaches out to us. His grace lifts those who cannot lift themselves.

Regards His Children as Precious

The psalmist relates a deep insight he gained through his brush with death and suffering: "Precious in the sight of the LORD is the death of his saints" (v. 15). This striking verse emphatically begins in Hebrew with the poignant term "precious," which suggests something costly, weighty, highly valued, and dear. The Lord does not regard lightly the mortal lives and deaths of his loved ones. He deeply treasures living relationships with them, and it costs him dearly when they suffer: "It *grieves* him when they die" (v. 15 NLT). The powerful image of *God grieving* shows us a Father in intimate relationship with his children and deeply caring for them! How utterly alien then to a biblical view of God would it be to imagine him as an impassive, emotionless deity, distant and detached from the feelings of our human weaknesses. No, God experiences anguish too as he grieves with us in our suffering and loss.

Indeed, the Bible tells us that God goes further yet and enters into our weak human estate, taking on the very likeness of mortal flesh in the person of Jesus. Completely in touch with every aspect of our existence—suffering; temptation, death—God in Christ is perfectly able to "sympathize with our weaknesses" (Heb. 4:15). The climax of the gospel story paints a vivid, cosmically colored picture of the pained anguish of God when Jesus, God's precious Son, was crucified. The earth itself shook, the midday skies darkened for three hours, and in the temple (the dwelling place of God's very presence), the curtain was torn from top to bottom! There could be no more startling and powerful picture of the broken heart of a grieving God. The death of his loved ones costs God dearly.

I know personally what a terrible toll deep grief takes on someone. As the curtain in the temple was torn from top to bottom when Jesus died, I felt like my whole being was being torn in two from top to bottom in the days and weeks following the death of Rachel. The pain and anguish were a whole body experience afflicting every aspect of my being. My spirit was shaken, my soul was torn, and my body sagged beneath the weight of my loss. Like presidents who age terribly during their time in office, I, too, found that my face told the story. The mirror clearly showed that years had found their way onto my face over a brief span of time. My spirit sagged as well. I have to admit that when my daughter died I felt deep down that there was nothing left for me here. In my darkest moments, I wanted to die too. Without one I loved and treasured so highly, I began to wonder what purpose there was in going on.

Direction for Going
on with Hope and Purpose

God's deliverance comes in different ways to each of us confronting suffering and death. For the psalmist here, it meant recovery—for a time. It is easy, therefore, to understand his thankful testimony since things got better for him. However, at this point, we must remember that Jesus' prayer in Gethsemane to be delivered from death was heard (Heb. 5:7), yet the answer included his death on Calvary. Both those prayers were similar and both were heard, yet differing pathways lay ahead on their journeys of faith. But both the psalmist and Jesus shared in common a bedrock trust in God: "May your will be done" (Matt. 26:42). Therefore, the common thread of going on, living in obedient faithfulness, stands as the challenge for us all, whatever pathway our deliverance might take.

TO LIVE WITH PURPOSE "BEFORE THE LORD" MEANS LIVING LIFE AS IF WALKING TOGETHER WITH GOD— EXPERIENCING ALL OF LIFE IN THE LIGHT OF HIS LOVING AND LIVING PRESENCE.

Walking with Purpose in the Land of the Living

After losing a loved one we can easily lose a sense of purpose for living on. The regular things that make up everyday life pale into insignificance. As time goes on we may wonder if we will ever laugh again, sing again, or know joy again. Just relating to people in the daily concourse of life can become a strain, something awkward and to be avoided. It is as if we have forgotten how to walk. People who have survived terrible crippling accidents may have legs so weakened from long periods of being bedridden that their muscles atrophy. When basic physical health returns, they must learn to walk again. The extreme pain of losing a loved one is like that, in a way. We can become so desolated and then isolated that we almost forget how to "walk" in this world.

In the psalmist's testimony, he thankfully recalls that the Lord has delivered his soul from death, poetically adding that his eyes were dried and his feet set solidly under him once again (v. 8). But most significantly, he concludes his thoughts with the phrase "*that* I may walk before the LORD in the land of the living" (v. 9). Here the psalmist passionately emphasizes that as long as he lives, his life "walk" will be *purposeful.* Having a sense of purpose for living, a God-centered and biblically conceived purpose, brought grace and power to his life—a crucial component in moving forward again after great struggle or loss.

The psalmist clarifies the indispensable starting point in walking again *with purpose* in the land of the living. It lies in the little phrase "before the LORD" (v. 9). Knowing that God's very presence is with him, the psalmist understands anew that his life's purpose only comes back into clear focus "before the Lord" who loves him and has never abandoned him. To live with purpose "before the Lord" means living life as if walking together with God—experiencing all of life in the light of his loving and living presence. Such a profound sense of God's real (if somewhat mysterious) presence carries with it both joy and challenge—an abiding inward assurance of his gracious loving care, but also a call to live well before the Holy One who walks beside us.

Who (and Whose) I Am before the Lord

As the psalmist contemplates a life lived before the Lord, he ponders plaintively, "How can I repay the LORD for all his goodness to me?"

(v. 12). He knows, of course, the inadequacy of any human attempts to compensate God for his saving work—no matter how fired up the intentions of a sincerely grateful heart. The reality is simply that there is no way to repay the Lord for his goodness and grace. How, then, do we respond? Humbled by the incredible reality that the God of the universe has chosen to reach out in love and grace to us, we can in return only love him, trust him completely, praise him, and serve him.

Most significantly, then, the psalmist truly knows who (and whose) he is before the Lord, humbly and simply calling himself "your servant" (v. 16). On one hand, his sense of identity as the Lord's servant points to his life's purpose in faithful service to his Master. Yet that service arises from a heart of gratitude since the Lord has freed him from his bonds. Here is the heartfelt sacrifice of a life given over in faithful servanthood to God—a *living sacrifice* to which all the rituals and offerings are but pointers (see Ps. 40:6–8; 51:17).

Jesus, the model "servant of the Lord," offered himself by saying, "Here I am … I have come to do your will, O God" (Heb. 10:7). Through Jesus' perfectly faithful and loving servanthood to God throughout his life, through his final, perfect sacrifice upon the cross, eternal salvation comes to all who love the Lord and place their lives in his hands as his servants. Truly, no greater identity for any person than that of the Lord's "servant" can ever exist! May we all, by his grace, come in faith to occupy such a precious position in the spiritual household of God.

What I Will Do before the Lord

The psalmist does, however, reveal what he will do as a servant in the household of God, now consciously walking "before the Lord."

First of all, he will set his soul at "rest" (v. 7). In light of God's deliverance and his abiding love for us, we may relax in his gracious care and presence. Years ago, graveyard stones were often inscribed with the letters *RIP* standing for "rest in peace." In light of the deliverance secured for us in Jesus, believers need not wait to rest in peace. We may do so now, refusing to be anxious or worried, instead trusting in the Lord to provide precisely what we need. Worry can consume us, but knowing that our eternal life is secure in Christ can bring a heavenly tranquility to every aspect of our transitory mortal lives. We may rest in peace, now and forevermore.

Second, the psalmist will give full credit to God for his gracious deliverance and presence in his life: "I will lift up the cup of salvation and call on the name of the LORD" (v. 13; parallel idea in v. 17). Literally, the psalmist may have taken a cup of wine and offered it as a libation of thanks to God (Num. 28:7, for example), then also in praise called out vocally the name of the Lord for all to hear. It picturesquely testified to a life owed completely to the one whose name he called out. Elsewhere in the Psalms, David, too, spoke of such an abundant cup of the Lord's gift of salvation: "My cup overflows" (Ps. 23:5). May we all,

> NO GREATER
> IDENTITY FOR ANY
> PERSON THAN THAT OF
> THE LORD'S "SERVANT"
> CAN EVER EXIST!

like the psalmist, testify plainly to the great gift of God's saving work in Jesus Christ, whose cup we raise in thanksgiving every time we take part in the Lord's Supper. As Paul wisely quotes Jeremiah, "Let him who boasts boast in the Lord" (1 Cor. 1:31).

In a similar way, the psalmist resolves to fulfill his vows—an unspecified reference to religious expressions of thanksgiving—before God's people (Ps. 116:14, 18–19). Keeping his promise in a visible manner serves as an inspiring testimony to others of God's grace and saving power. Ultimately, the rituals and sacrifices had their real value in the way they witnessed to the relationship he had with God. Such a witness needs to be heard in the "courts of the house of the LORD" (v. 19).

Our daughter's memorial service was held in a large church building. Over a thousand people came. School buses brought kids from her local public middle school. Whole athletic teams came, and many supportive family, school, and church friends came to express their support and care. Throughout the service, Rachel's relationship with Christ and her kindness to others were a recurring testimonial theme. The witness of her life, a life owed to God, continued to bear fruit even after her death. In a chest in our home are letters from people who came to the service. In one such letter from someone we did not even know, a family expressed their condolences but went on to express their thanksgiving. Following the service, you see, the whole family had given their lives to Christ, desiring to have the kind of relationship with God that Rachel had. The flame of her life, placed in the midst of God's people, kindled hope and faith in others, blazing on beyond her years in this mortal sphere. Indeed, as the psalmist said, "Precious in the sight of the LORD is the death of his saints" (v. 15). As God himself so treasures his godly loved ones, so, too, will we.

Where Is the Hope?

Hope reaches out to us powerfully through the testimony of this humble psalmist. That God keeps on hearing our cries in the midst of suffering and loss tells us how much he loves us. He never abandons us. That he even "grieves" with us shows us how deeply he treasures relationship with us as his precious ones. But in the final analysis, hope comes alive most vividly as the psalmist's testimony calls us to look forward to God's grace and saving power extended to all people in Jesus Christ—the precious "Servant of the Lord" whose death and resurrection bring eternal healing and life to all who trust in him and walk faithfully "before the Lord." Therein lies the greatest hope of all.

"HERE IS MY HEART, LORD ..."

Lord, when I've been in dire straits in life, the testimonies of people do touch me—sometimes positively and helpfully ... sometimes not.

God, when I've come face-to-face with death—my own or a dearly loved one's—then I realize more clearly that ...

When I'm really low in spirit, Lord, other people sometimes can upset me because ...

Knowing that you always "hear" me, God, gives me a sense that you ...

When I feel small, insignificant, and just "simplehearted," and life's difficulties are complex and beyond me, remind me, Lord, that you ...

The verse "Precious in the sight of the LORD is the death of his saints" (v. 15) tells me that you, Lord ...

Thinking of you, God, as "grieving" for those you love reminds me that ...

Lord, in light of your Word here in Psalm 116, I can see that my purpose in life ...

Having my personal identity as your "servant," God, means that I ...

Lord, I can see that wisely and sensitively sharing the testimony of my faith journey through great suffering could be really helpful to others. Help me to ...

Chapter 3

SORROWS UNENDING, HOPE UNDYING

—❧ LAMENTATIONS ❧—

*Devastated by unspeakable loss and filled with dark,
foreboding emotions, we sit and wonder what to do with it
all. How empty and deserted I feel! How could this have
happened? How can I go on? The "hows" of grievous loss pile
on us, and our broken hearts falter. Surprisingly, God's help
comes through songs of sorrow—poetry of death that never
passes away but puts us on the pathway of healing and hope.*

Defining moments mark the landscape of our lives, casting their
light (or shadow) over nations, generations, families, homes, and
individuals. Such pivotal events—whether major world events or private, personal, and family events—etch themselves into our innermost
consciousness, impacting us forever.

In 2003, the space shuttle *Columbia* disintegrated in the sky, and
watchers worldwide looked on horrified, yet transfixed. In a fiery flash
the lives of the crew exploded before myriads of disbelieving eyewitnesses.
Who can forget this unnerving sight? Certainly not their families and
loved ones. They were marked forever.

The movie *Saving Private Ryan* begins with the poignant scene of an aged veteran marching painfully and slowly on a path by a seashore. As he passes along row upon row of white grave markers at the Normandy cemetery—his family trailing anxiously behind him—he stops finally and falls to his knees, breaking down in tears before one particular white grave marker cross. Here the soldier who had saved his life lay buried, one among thousands of heroes who gave their lives on D-day, June 6, 1944, and the days thereafter to free Europe from Nazi tyranny. Through the life and sacrifice of this one man, he, too, was marked forever.

IN THE SHADOW OF DESTRUCTION AND DEPORTATION, OF DISILLUSIONMENT AND DISCOURAGEMENT, GOD WAS NOT SILENT.

Someone need only say the numbers "9/11" to communicate the tragedy of the terrorist attack on the World Trade Center in 2001. This horrific event has had a ripple effect throughout the United States and the world, an impact that is changing world history. Through the despicable act of some evil men, the lives of those who lost loved ones that day—and the life of the world at large—was scarred forever.

Defining moments—those unexpected, unprepared-for disasters—affect us as citizens of a larger world but also at an intensely personal level.

Such a defining moment slammed itself into our lives with an unwelcome phone call telling us to come to the hospital immediately. We feared the worst on that drive to the hospital, and once we arrived, the chaplain told us kindly but simply that our pride and joy—our beautiful and beloved daughter of only fourteen—had died of a heart attack. The sheer shock was almost unendurable and I nearly passed out, fainting into a grievous grayness. Over the ensuing hours and days, events tore into our souls and forced us to reckon with the inescapable reality of our incredible loss. There was a memorial service and a graveside ceremony ... an empty, quiet bedroom ... a pair of new shoes in a box, just purchased, never to be worn. In that terrible quiet of an undisturbed bed and unworn shoes, one unavoidable question came again and again: What do we do now? How do we respond? We, too, were marked forever by our great loss—and by our response to it.

The initial shock from a great loss has an almost numbing effect, followed by a series of situations in which its awful, painful reality gradually sinks in. Though we may employ a variety of avoidance techniques to deny or delay reckoning with it, its reality will sooner or later come home fully. What then will we do? How will we respond? Thankfully, God's Word guides us to healthy and even hopeful avenues of response in faith.

POETRY OF DEATH
THAT NEVER PASSES AWAY

One of the most monumental and painful losses Israel experienced happened in the year 587 BC when the Babylonians, under King Nebuchadnezzar, attacked Jerusalem. They slaughtered many, laid waste to the city, and destroyed its pride and joy—the great Solomonic temple. What was yet worse, the Babylonians led the Jewish people off into exile as captives in Babylon. There was loss of lives, home, family, and country; loss of heart; and perhaps even loss of faith and hope. This dark chapter in the history of Israel, a major defining moment in the Old Testament, marked the Jewish people forever. The key question: What would be their response?

One surprisingly hopeful response, which has ministered to believers ever since, comes through a collection of five poems or songs of death (known as dirges) penned by a likely eyewitness commemorating these terrible events—the Lamentations of the prophet Jeremiah. In the shadow of destruction and deportation, of disillusionment and discouragement, God was not silent but spoke through Jeremiah's songs of death to hearts broken and desperately reaching out for hope. And the songs still speak today to those seeking a pathway back to hope.

THE IMAGE OF A HEART "POURED OUT" TO GOD VIVIDLY PICTURES THE COMPLETE AND UNRESTRAINED FLOW OF OUR TRUEST FEELINGS TO GOD, LIKE WATER SMOOTHLY FLOWING OUT OF A VASE.

Interestingly, careful study of Scripture often reveals structural features that aid in understanding what the author is trying to communicate. For instance, the five independent poems share some intriguingly common features that carry meaning. Four of the five poems (Lam. 1—4) are acrostics, each verse or section of verses (Lam. 3 is arranged in triplets, sixty-six instead of twenty-two verses) beginning with the next letter of the Hebrew alphabet. Through what looks like a clever literary trick, Jeremiah may be trying to say that here in these poems is the "A to Z" of their grief and loss, exhaustively expressed and with nothing left out. Such a nothing-held-back approach surely seems to be what happens throughout these pained expressions of grief. More obviously, the poems share common themes of loss and sorrow throughout—abandonment, anger, hopelessness, vengefulness, no sense of comfort, guilt and judgment, regret, and even darker emotions and experiences.

Yet, perhaps most significantly, Jeremiah begins his first poem and two others (Lam. 2, 4) with the loaded exclamatory word *How!* For example: "How the gold has lost its luster, the fine gold become dull!" (4:1). This pregnant little word captures the extreme pain and indirectly suggests the heartrending questions underlying the poems: "How could this have happened? How can we go on living? How can I express what I am feeling? How can I still believe?"[1] How fitting that the word *how* itself is the title of this book in the Hebrew Bible, though the more thematic Greek title lies behind our English Bible title "Lamentations." But the single term *how* captures perfectly in poetry the expression of pain and the implied question of "How then shall we respond?"

Notably, on the ninth of Ab (a Jewish month around July/August) every year, Jewish people around the world read the book of Lamentations in synagogues. Appropriate to its historical background in the fall of Jerusalem, Lamentations sets the spiritual tone for a sort of Jewish Memorial Day—a day of fasting and mourning, remembrance, confession, and contrition, and a call to trust God anew for future mercies. Rabbi Ginsberg poignantly writes, "We do well to recite Lamentations … to recall not only the grief of the national catastrophe, but the source from which our people drew the strength to recover from it."[2] These are the two basic movements of the heart of a believer when facing great loss: (1) recall the grief, and (2) recall also the source of strength people of faith like Jeremiah drew upon to recover.

POUR YOUR HEART OUT LIKE WATER TO GOD!

Jeremiah feels a passionate need to express his pain, to tell someone, and so he cries out to God. In chapter one alone, he begs God four times to "look" and "see" his suffering and distress (vv. 9, 11–12, 20). He wants and needs to be heard, and he trusts God to be there for him as a safe outlet for his unrestrained anguish. Jeremiah not only models a broken heart open fully to God, but also encourages others—us—to join him in such a vulnerable baring of our souls before a loving and faithful God. In picturesque terms he urges, "Pour out your heart like water in the presence of the Lord" (2:19). Almost consumed by his pain, he says his "eyes fail from weeping" and his "heart is poured out on the ground" (2:11) and goes on to encourage people to "let your tears flow like a river day and night" (2:18). The image of a heart "poured out" to God vividly pictures the complete and unrestrained flow of our truest feelings to God, like water smoothly flowing out of a vase.

The five poems of Lamentations (best read in one sitting) virtually flood us with a tidal wave of sorrow and grief. They are not an easy or light read. The major key of this poetic symphony is sorrow and pain, a tone that dominates these songs of death almost unrelentingly. We are nearly overwhelmed as the majority of the poems' lines explore the vast ocean of human feelings of loss and grief, each poem from its own perspective returning again and again to common themes: abandonment, aloneness, hopelessness, anger, no sense of comfort, guilt, regret, the lost ability to be happy or dance, sitting in silence with dirt on the head, a sense of being cursed, dreams now gone, unable to rest, loss of security, no energy … and the sad list goes on and on. A sense of being "unblessed" washes over the soul, leaving mostly the somber dominant tones of desperation and desolation. Jeremiah left no stone of sorrow unturned. He truly poured out his heart like water in the presence of the Lord.

Teddy Roosevelt cut a monumental swath through American history, joining the other presidential giants on Mount Rushmore. As a young man, he married the love of his life, and together they charged into life with characteristic vigor. Full of talent, great potential, huge vision, daring and a dreamer's soul, "TR" grasped life by the horns. His beloved wife's pregnancy brought great excitement, joy, and anticipation. But as time for the birth approached, his mother took ill. Sadly enough, on

Valentine's Day that year his mother died of typhoid—but the tragedy doubled when on the very same day his wife died in childbirth. Roosevelt was a diarist and was seldom short of words, but on that day he entered into his diary just an *X* and nothing else. The next day he entered a solitary line: "All the light has gone out of my life." After a short time of deep grief, he never mentioned his wife again, never again wrote about her in his diary at all. Some years later he counseled a friend who had suffered a similar loss to put it utterly out of his mind and never to mention the loved one again.

Though we continued attending church after the loss of our daughter, I must admit it took a long time for me to be able to sing out loud. A quiet, reflective, and familiar place like church can be a hard place for someone grieving a loved one so associated with the faith and life of the church. For nearly a year, I just stood during worship and let the music and words minister to me. Some people, I learned, wondered why I wasn't singing. After all, shouldn't someone of faith just "get over it" and "move on" with life?

JEREMIAH'S POEMS TAKE US IN A VERY DIFFERENT DIRECTION, TO LEARN THE LESSONS OF GRIEF BY REMEMBERING OUR SORROW WITH UNFLINCHING HONESTY WITHIN THE EMBRACE OF AN UNDERSTANDING FATHER GOD.

The reality is that you don't just get over it, as the misguided Roosevelt similarly suggested to his grieving friend. A critical part of the healing process is precisely what Jeremiah calls us to do, each in our own way and time: Pour out your heart like water to God. TR's guidance was to put it behind you, to forget about it, to just move on and get over it. But Jeremiah's poems take us in a very different direction, to learn the lessons of grief by remembering our sorrow with unflinching honesty within the embrace of an understanding Father God. Nothing should be hidden, nothing held back. We are free in love to be seared souls abandoned to God, free to cry out to him who will walk with us patiently through our pain. Let us pursue the path of the poet, not the president, and pour out our hearts like water in the presence of the Lord!

In his second poem, Jeremiah poses a leading question that underlies all five poems: "Your wound is as deep as the sea. *Who can heal you?*" (2:13). Jeremiah does not look to the nation's leaders or even religious leaders, for they came up short. Obviously, Israel's enemies gloated over Israel's sorry state. No, Jeremiah knows there is nowhere else to turn for healing but to the Lord.

PUT YOUR HOPE
ONLY AND FINALLY IN GOD!

One of the great Scottish regiments is known simply as the Black Watch, and the Black Watch tartan remains one of my favorites. Dark, rich colors course through its weave with far fewer threads of bright colors. However, the effect is that the bright colors stand out all the more because of that darker, rich background. All together they produce a particularly rich and beautiful weave.

Lamentations has a Black Watch sort of feel to it—many dark colors but only a few bright ones. Yet those threads of bright hope are interwoven into the faith fabric of this collection of Jeremiah's poems and stand out all the more as a result of their scarcity. Some of the poems carry only a hint of hope within them (Lam. 1—2; 4). But the bright colors of hope and faith stand out most vividly in Lamentations 3:18–32.

In Job 13:15, following the loss of virtually everything precious to him, Job utters one of the most famous lines in all Scripture: "Though he slay me, *yet* will I hope in him." That "yet" of authentically yielded faith in God finds a vibrant echo in Lamentations 3:18–32—an oasis of hope in the sea of grief. In these incredible poetic stanzas, Jeremiah never loses sight of his life context of affliction, bitterness, gall, and the downcast soul within him.

> Yet this I call to mind and therefore I have hope: Because of the LORD's great love we are not consumed, for his compassions never fail. They are new every morning; great is your faithfulness. I say to myself, "The LORD is my portion; therefore I will wait for him." The LORD is good to those whose hope is in him, to the one who seeks him; it is good to wait quietly for the salvation of the LORD. (3:21–26)

Why does Jeremiah *yet* hope, trust, and wait on the Lord? Lamentations 3:22–24 points us to God's "great love," a term in Hebrew (*hesed*) that means a loyal love that sticks by his people. Furthermore, that loyal love unfolds to us in God's unfailing "compassions"—a Hebrew term from the word for a womb—a vivid picture of the Lord's gentle yet intense concern for his children. Such a loving disposition of God toward us is inexhaustible, full and new every morning. Little wonder that Jeremiah exclaims in praise: "Great is your faithfulness!" The classic hymn, taken from this passage, accents the unchanging constancy of God's love and mercy: "There is no shadow of turning with Thee. Thou changest not. Thy compassions they fail not. As Thou hast been, Thou forever wilt be." That same hymn also highlights the fact that God's unchanging, compassionate love furnishes solid ground for those hopeful ones reaching out again to the future: "Strength for today and bright hope for tomorrow."

Jeremiah tells himself in 3:24, "The LORD is my portion." Another version puts it helpfully, "Yahweh is all I have" (NJB). Peter verbalized that final, utter faith dependence when Jesus asked him if he wanted to quit following him: "Lord, to whom shall we go? You have the words of eternal life" (John 6:68). The Lord Jesus, Peter realized, was his "portion" and all he would ever ultimately need. God's very mercy, loyal love, and compassion became flesh in the person of Jesus Christ, "the same yesterday and today and forever" (Heb. 13:8).

WE ARE FREE IN LOVE TO BE SEARED SOULS ABANDONED TO GOD, FREE TO CRY OUT TO HIM WHO WILL WALK WITH US PATIENTLY THROUGH OUR PAIN.

The final poem (Lam. 5), though still governed by expressions of grief—"Joy is gone from our hearts; our dancing has turned to mourning" (v. 15)—contains a triad of Jeremiah's powerful pleas of hope as he addresses God: "*Remember*, O LORD, what has happened to us" (v. 1); "*Restore* us to yourself, O LORD" (v. 21); *Renew* our days as of old" (v. 21). Here is a prayer of faith and hope in the midst of hardship: *Remember our heartache, restore us to relationship with you, and renew our lives through your healing power!* On this note of hope for the future, Lamentations ends.

Where Is the Hope?

Rabbi Ginsberg issued a pointed challenge when he said that "learning the lesson of Lamentations may well hold the secret to the nation's survival."[3] What was true for Israel remains true for us today. Indeed, learning and putting into practice the lesson of Lamentations may be the key to our survival as individual Christians, as families, and as churches. But it is a secret experienced only as in faith we *pour our hearts out like water to God* and *put our hope only and finally in him.* The apostle Peter understood the deep humility necessary to utter such dependence upon God in the midst of hardship and captured well the spirit of Lamentations when he said, "Humble yourselves, therefore, under God's mighty hand, that he may lift you up in due time. Cast all your anxiety on him because he cares for you" (1 Peter 5:6–7).

"HERE IS MY HEART, LORD …"

God, I desperately need to express to you what's going on in my heart right now, to say just how I really feel about my loss, but I'm afraid because …

Lord, I have some "hows" of my loss I really need to let out, so here they are: "How …!" "How …?" "How …!" "How …?"

Oh, Father God, some of the brokenhearted feelings I see "poured out like water" in Lamentations really feel familiar to my own experience of loss, especially …

I'd have to admit, Lord, that I've experienced people's well-meant, but hurtful, "Get over it" kinds of advice when someone …

… So, Lord, help me to respond by …

It is hard for me, Lord, but I can see some bright threads of hope and grace woven into my loss, such as …

For me, Lord, knowing that your love and compassions never run out and are "new every morning" means ...

God, when I hear Peter's words in 1 Peter 5:6–7—"Humble yourselves, therefore, under God's mighty hand, that he may lift you up in due time. Cast all your anxiety on him because he cares for you"— I am challenged to ...

... But those inspired words also encourage me greatly because ...

Chapter 4

VOICES OF COMFORT
IN THE DESERT

ISAIAH 40

*Abandoned and alone, frail and failing, hanging on by a
thread. All seems lost. Is there any hope for me in this
lifeless desert exiled from all I once held dear? Yet in the
stifling silence of hopelessness a voice sounds out to my
heart. Yes, I hear it—a voice, a comforting voice, calling
out ... crying out ... shouting out....*

Comfort, comfort my people, says your God.

—Isaiah 40:1

I n the first days following Rachel's death, the sheer shock was like a
concussion of my whole person. What feeling I did have was utterly
devoted to the pain piercing my soul—a pain that found voice alter-
nately in anger, survivor guilt, and dull despair.

The prophet Isaiah and his contemporaries knew that same terrible
pain. The pressing question in their day was, "Is there any hope for us?"
Their very lives had been brutally torn from them when the Jewish

nation was conquered and the people forcibly relocated to distant Babylon, where they lived in gloomy exile.

The psalmist captures their mournful spirit: "By the rivers of Babylon we sat and wept when we remembered Zion" (Ps. 137:1).

Remembering the grievous loss of what they held dearest, these exiles—now alone, homeless, and helpless—despaired of their future and resigned themselves to a desolate, dismal destiny.

WE BEAR RESPONSIBILITY TO CLEAR AWAY WHATEVER ROADBLOCKS MIGHT HINDER GOD'S COMFORT.

This sense of "exile" captures well my own feeling of loss and dislocation when my daughter died. What was most precious to me was now gone. Overwhelmed by my own helplessness and sorrow, like the psalmist I simply sat and wept as I *remembered*. Clear, sharp remembering only etched the feelings of "exile" more deeply in my soul as the sense of alienation from life, home, and blessing threatened to crush me. Was there any hope? Or was resigned despair the only response left?

CALL TO COMFORT

Isaiah 40 speaks prophetically to people awash in a dark mood of despair and hopelessness nearly forty years after the exile. It begins with Isaiah's call from God to *comfort* the exiled, to actively intervene. God gives the command twice (v. 1), showing the desperate need for this comfort. There remain hope and help from God. He has not abandoned us but will intervene on our behalf! But how?

This message of comfort from God was "good tidings"—hopeful news in the midst of bad times (v. 9). Isaiah was to "speak tenderly" (v. 2) to God's exiled people, a phrase that quite literally means to speak "to the heart." This calls for deep sensitivity to the soul of the sufferer. Isaiah was also told to "proclaim" to them that their exile would not go on forever, a proclaiming that points to strength of conviction in what is being said. Together, "speak tenderly" and "proclaim" show that the prophetic voice of comfort comes from *both* a heartfelt sensitivity and a strong faith stance.

Recently, I received a call from a former student now serving as the pastor of a local church. A well-loved parent from his congregation had tragically died in a traffic accident; and now, as is the case with all of us, the question of "What do I say?" loomed large. Oddly, a Christian counselor told the pastor to be sure not to "throw Scripture at" the bereaved spouse and family. After a brief debate with the counselor, the pastor wondered about the wisdom of such advice. To be sure, no one should "throw" Scripture indiscriminately at anyone, but such misplaced paranoia about using Scripture will only muffle the voice of God's comfort they so

NO MATTER HOW ALONE WE MAY FEEL, THE LORD HAS NOT ABANDONED US BUT ALWAYS REMAINS THERE FOR US, POWERFUL TO HELP AND TO SAVE.

desperately need to hear. Over the phone I shared God's message in Isaiah 40, a word God's Spirit later used through this pastor to bring timely hope and comfort to that heartbroken family.

We all need to hear such voices of comfort, tenderly speaking to heartache yet brimming with a firm trust in God. Three distinct *voices* of comfort ring out from Isaiah 40 with messages from God that bring hope to the heartbroken whose sense of "exile" has all but overwhelmed their souls.

VOICE OF COMFORT: "HELP IS ON THE WAY!" (ISA. 40:3–5)

Turn to the Lord

The first voice of prophecy foresees God's coming and calls his people to prepare the way for his arrival, literally to clear away any obstacle(s) that might interfere with his coming—and his comforting. In a sublimely poetic picture of valleys, mountains, and rugged places being smoothed and made passable, Isaiah paints a vision of unhindered access for God. As with the exiled Jewish refugees long ago, we bear responsibility to clear away whatever roadblocks might hinder God's comfort. We, too, must heed the call to prepare the way.

Every gospel records John the Baptist quoting these words of Isaiah (vv. 3–5) to describe his ministry in readying people for the coming ministry of the Lord Jesus: "I am the voice of one calling in the desert, 'Make straight the way for the Lord'" (John 1:23). John was in the spiritual road-construction business, and he knew people needed to "prepare" for the Lord's coming, to put aside all personal obstacles so that his healing salvation would have a clear road into their lives. His message bore a singular keynote that explained how to prepare the way: *"Repent!"* Though an old-fashioned word, it still resonates with the dual movement of its call to turn away from obstacles that isolate us from God and to turn back to the Lord.

It may seem a curious and inappropriate thing to say to someone feeling profound loss, but the call to repent—to turn to the Lord—is the important first step in experiencing a divine comfort that begins the healing process.

It is easy to become so wrapped up in pain and loss that God gets relegated to the sidelines of our attention. The prayers and spiritual counsel going on all around us can become just so many words bouncing ineffectively off the harsh reality of our loss. And the net result is that we do not turn to the very person of the Lord—the "God of all comfort" (2 Cor. 1:3).

A couple of days after Rachel's death a Christian friend came by, and though he spoke compassionately, he also challenged me by asking simply: "John, have you seen God's grace at all?" Frankly, I hadn't thought much about grace. He then left a copy of C. S. Lewis's *A Grief Observed*, a book I had read long ago and in a very different time of life. In Lewis's distinctive style he interacts with himself, God, and the reader concerning the loss of his wife, wrestling mightily with his own anguish. In the end Lewis finds himself looking again to the God of love, grace, mercy, and comfort—and rediscovers his faith in a new life context.

Pain had become the center of my existence, while God and his grace were all but excluded. The biggest obstacle that needed to be cleared away, preparing the way for the Lord to bring his grace and comfort, was my self-absorption. Lewis's little book helped my wife and me give expression to a fuller range of responses to our own loss. More important, we found ourselves turning to the Lord once again and rediscovering his comfort, love, and grace—sufficient even to our heartbroken souls.

Travel through the Desert with Him

Interestingly now, Isaiah locates the road upon which God comes to the exhausted Jewish exiles. It is precisely in the desert wilderness that the royal road will run. For the record, the road back from Babylon to Jerusalem would normally have avoided the direct path through the harsh Arabian Desert, traversing the easier route along the Fertile Crescent around the desert back to Israel. Notably, the pathway of God's comfort, however, lies in the desert wilderness itself.

Isaiah's prophetic voice of comfort here surely speaks to more than mere geography. It is in the desert, a poignant symbol of the Israelites' own dry and lifeless estate, that the voice of comfort announces the coming of God's road to recovery. The road back home runs through the desert. It does not detour around, nor does it approach the desert and turn away, as if denying its existence. No, God comes in comfort to these exiles precisely where their lives are driest and most difficult and their sense of loss most profound.

ACCEPTING THE FRAILTY AND FUTILITY OF OUR OWN SPEECH AND OUR OWN STRENGTH IS THE NECESSARY STARTING POINT FOR EXPERIENCING COMFORT, FOR ONLY THEN WILL WE LOOK BEYOND OURSELVES.

Deserts and wildernesses come in many shapes and sizes. The desertlike "exile" of grief and loss often carries with it a sense of dislocation, guilt, homelessness, despair about the future, and uncertainty about how to even go on living. Typically, we try to turn away from such searing pain altogether or take easier Fertile Crescent–like routes around it. But the pain remains undiminished by either our denials or our avoidance. No, the desert must—and will—be crossed.

Now, if the road home to recovery runs in and right through our deserts, Isaiah holds up the hope that God himself will accompany us along the way back home. When Isaiah prophesies that God's "glory" will be revealed, he is saying that God's own shining and wonderful presence will be known by us on that deserted wilderness road. We are not alone there, but joined by

One who will walk alongside us and who is completely able to deliver us safely. No matter how alone we may feel, the Lord has not abandoned us but always remains there for us, powerful to help and to save. His presence and help are on the way and sure to come—precisely at our point of need.

Though my family experienced God's comforting presence and help—his glory—in personal and direct ways, other people observed us in our wilderness experience. That "all mankind together will see" God's glory (v. 5) points to a world watching to see how God helps his people—an indirect "seeing" but a seeing of God's glory nevertheless.

Our memory chest of mementos of our daughter's life contains a variety of precious items, but one letter stands out in particular. It tells of a family of four who attended the memorial service for Rachel, heard and observed what was said and done, and saw a piece of what, I believe, was the glory of God—his real presence and help in Rachel's life and now in ours. The letter went on to explain with simplicity and heartfelt gratitude how their whole family as a result now trusted God with their lives for now and forever. An oasis of glory, hope, and peace in the midst of a desert of grief and loss.

VOICE OF COMFORT: "HIS WORD STANDS FOREVER!" (ISA. 40:6–8)

Isaiah's second voice of comfort starts with a command and a question. On one hand, this message of comfort *must* be cried out, but that immediately begs the question: "What shall I cry?" This honest question hits the nail squarely on the head when confronted by grief and loss, for what words are sufficient for such times as these? Though we feel something has to be said, we are awkwardly muted in the face of reality, overwhelmed by the despair of not knowing what to say.

Face-to-Face with Futility

Drawing on the common, poetic metaphor of grass and flowers, this voice of comfort begins with an honest recognition of human impermanence and impotence. As the spring wildflowers and grass burst colorfully onto the landscape, so, too, they soon wither away beneath the sizzling blasts of sirocco winds blowing out of the desert. Like nothing else in human experience, grief and loss bring us face-to-face with mortality.

Accepting the frailty and futility of our own speech and our own strength is the necessary starting point for experiencing comfort, for only then will we look beyond ourselves. King David understood this well. In Psalm 39:5–7 he writes, "You have made my days a mere handbreadth; the span of my years is as nothing before you. Each man's life is but a breath. Man is a mere phantom as he goes to and fro: He bustles about, but only in vain; he heaps up wealth, not knowing who will get it. But now, Lord, what do I look for? My hope is in you." When we grieve, life takes on a grayness, a hazy feel of unreality. There is a profound awareness of life's transience. In light of human frailty and its fleeting life span, David looks beyond himself for hope and sustenance—and so must we.

TO BE EFFECTIVE AT THE HIGHEST LEVEL, WORDS OF COMFORT MUST BE BAPTIZED IN THE DEEP WATERS OF THE WORD OF GOD.

Forever-Enduring Word of God

Having now acknowledged human weakness, in emphatic contrast Isaiah decisively declares, "But the word of our God stands forever."

God's promises, truths, and his very person are not subject to the inevitable decay the world and its creatures experience, but rather his Word endures and abides eternally valid and effective. Nothing can void it—no matter how terrible the plight. God's Word persists permanently and powerfully.

It is no accident that this section of Isaiah's prophecy concludes in Isaiah 55:10–11 with an invitation to trust God's Word: "As the rain and the snow come down from heaven, and do not return to it without watering the earth and making it bud and flourish, so that it yields seed for the sower and bread for the eater, so is my word that goes out from my mouth: It will not return to me empty, but will accomplish what I desire and achieve the purpose for which I sent it."

God's Word—in Scripture and in his person—remains utterly reliable and trustworthy in accomplishing his purposes in relationships with humankind. It is never empty, but always effective. Isaiah, therefore, points us to the only eternally secure and stable source of comfort, God's Word.

As Christians we know that God's Word took form in our world in the person of Jesus—"the Word became flesh" (John 1:14). To know Jesus the Word is to know God's Word. Hebrews 1:2 straightforwardly states that God has spoken to us by his Son. In Jesus we see the enduring and eternally reliable Word of God, always there for us. In Hebrews 13:7 the biblical author calls us to remember great spiritual leaders who share God's Word with us. However, these beloved servants of the Lord do pass away. Jesus, on the other hand, "is the same yesterday and today and forever" (Heb. 13:8). Our hope must ever and always be rooted solely in the unchanging and unchangeable Lord himself, for all else will fade away.

As he saw his own earthly life passing away, the apostle Paul gave one final charge in his last letter to his protégé Timothy: "Preach the Word" (2 Tim. 4:2). How easily we slide toward giving counsel in everything but the direct and plain words of Scripture. To be effective at the highest level, words of comfort must be baptized in the deep waters of the Word of God. In a world where everything shifts and fades, where we debate the meaning of the word *is*, where values vary and morals move at human whim, where too often we recline on couches of cultural correctness, the question inevitably arises: What will stand? What will last? What can we count on? Only one answer suffices: His Word endures forever.

We will only find true comfort when we, along with David, turn away from ourselves and cry out: "O Lord, my hope is in you!"

VOICE OF COMFORT: "HERE IS YOUR GOD!" (ISA. 40:9–31)

The third and final voice of comfort in Isaiah 40 fearlessly and firmly shouts to the exile a singular prophetic message (v. 9): "Here is your God!" Look carefully at the God in whom we hope. Here is the God of all comfort! Such a clarion call to remember just who our God is arises out of a deep need, for in long, dark moments the one who grieves may well wonder if God is able to help—and whether he cares to help. Pointing to the very person of God, the prophetic voice of comfort answers such questions with a resounding "Yes!" on both counts.

Isaiah casts two pictures of God in 40:10–11 that vividly portray God as more than able both to help and to care lovingly for his hurting people. In 40:10, Isaiah calls us to see God as the *Sovereign Lord*, eminently powerful both to rule and to reward. There is no doubt that this Lord is able to help. Then, too, in 40:11, Isaiah further calls us to see God as the *Sovereign Shepherd* who tenderly cares for all his flock, his own people. A crisis of confidence often comes to those who have experienced great loss, but if we remember who our God is—that he is able to help and that he does care—we can experience his fullest comfort. He can help. He cares.

Sovereign Lord (vv. 10, 12–26)

Isaiah's vision of God as Sovereign Lord (announced in 40:10) unfolds in poetic imagery (vv. 12–26). Throughout the passage Isaiah establishes one clear point: God's grace and comfort are available because he is powerfully able to help—and none can interfere with his aid.

Drawing out the theme of measurement, Isaiah depicts the Lord's sovereign power as *immeasurable* (vv. 12–17). Whether we consider vast oceans or heavens or the earth itself, it is God who measures everything. He sizes up and weighs the unfathomable elements of the entire universe as if but a tiny thing to him—taking it all in by the span of his hand! Further, none can take the measure of God. The very thought is absurd. Even whole nations—including Babylon, which might presume to oppose the Lord—are so insignificant as to be "a drop in a bucket ... less than nothing" (vv. 15, 17).

NONE CAN COMPARE TO GOD'S GREAT POWER AND MIGHTY STRENGTH— OR STAND IN THE WAY OF HIS HELP AND COMFORT TO HIS PEOPLE.

Isaiah then describes the Lord's sovereign power as *incomparable* (vv. 18–26). With oppressive Babylon in mind, Isaiah now compares the greatest potential rivals to the Lord. First, Isaiah explores the idol-making process with careful attention to detail, understating the absurd reality that craftsmen must labor mightily to make these gods and make sure they do not fall over (vv. 18–20). Isaiah does not directly mock or criticize such idols. It is so obviously foolish that the mere description speaks for itself. Next, the prophet gazes at the glittering stars in the sky that supposedly determined every person's fate—the astral cult of Marduk, the sun god, was prominent in Babylon—and recalls that God created all the heavens (vv. 21–22, 26). When the Lord calls the roll for the myriad stars, naming each one, they all show up right on time! Finally, Isaiah considers the world's great princes' powers as but so much dust in the wind, swept away like chaff as the Lord blows on them (vv. 23–24). Isaiah sums it up concerning the Lord's power: "'To whom will you compare me? Or who is my equal?' says the Holy One" (v. 25). Clearly, none can compare to God's great power and mighty strength—or stand in the way of his help and comfort to his people.

WHEN WE TRUST IN HIS LOVE, WE EXPERIENCE A MIRACULOUS EXCHANGE—HIS STRENGTH FOR OUR WEAKNESS.

Sovereign Shepherd (vv. 11, 27–31)

Because the prophet recognizes how abandoned an exile feels, he acknowledges this complaint (v. 27) and returns to the theme of knowing God as Sovereign Shepherd (v. 11). Far from disregarding their hurt, God is like a shepherd to them and shows especially tender care for the most vulnerable of the flock, the lambs and mothering ewes. The imagery of God gathering in his arms, carrying close to the heart, and leading gently (v. 11) points to God's hands-on care. He involves himself in our protection, provision, and progress.

Isaiah points to God's *grace* as he gives strength to the weary and stumbling sufferer. When struck down by loss, no one is invincible or untouchable. Even the seemingly tireless youth loses his energy and cramps up in pain (vv. 29–30). Every one of us desperately needs God's grace to go on in life's journey.

Curiously, however, we go onward by waiting. To "wait on the LORD" (v. 31 NLT) hardly means sitting back passively, but rather it means an eagerly expectant attitude of hope focused on the Lord himself. To "hope in the LORD" means we embrace life again empowered by God. When we trust in his love, we experience a miraculous exchange—his strength for our weakness.

Now whether flying, running, or just walking, by God's grace we move forward again at whatever pace and on whatever pathway the Lord wisely directs us. Oddly, the triad of flying, running, and walking (40:31) climaxes with the slowest of the three—perhaps a subtle sign that even painstakingly slow strides do take us forward—the movement of hope.

God's shepherding care and involvement in our lives to protect, provide, and help us progress reached its perfect expression in Jesus, the Good Shepherd. Jesus' sacrificial love on the cross—"I lay down my life" (John 10:11–18)—is the pinnacle of God's personal involvement in our suffering and sinful estate. His care stands unquestioned. And the Good Shepherd Jesus' promise of security for his sheep remains unchallenged: "I give them eternal life, and they shall never perish; no one can snatch them out of my hand" (10:28). In Jesus the prophecy of the Sovereign Shepherd's comfort reaches its perfect fulfillment. Here is your God!

Where Is the Hope?

When in the desert of grief and loss we cry out for God to hear us in our pain, he calls out to us with these prophetic voices of hope and comfort. His help comes to us exiles in the midst of our deserts, precisely at our point of need, and we must turn to him. Then, too, his Word of love remains eternally reliable and trustworthy, even when all else seems empty and fading. Finally, his own person in sovereign, loving power is always available to those who hope in him. These three voices of comfort together tell us that hope lies solely in the Lord, the God of all comfort. Isaiah fittingly concludes his prophetic message about the Lord's comfort by anticipating the fulfillment of that comfort in 52:9: "Burst into songs of joy together, you ruins of Jerusalem, for the LORD has comforted his people." So, for us David's words still speak: "But now, Lord, what do I look for? My hope is in you" (Ps. 39:7).

"HERE IS MY HEART, LORD ..."

Lord, I identify with the psalmist who, in exile by the Babylonian rivers, wept as he remembered the past and grieved. In my pain, I, too, have experienced an "exile." I sometimes weep as I remember ...

For your comfort to reach me, Lord, I know I have to prepare the way. If there are roadblocks I've put up that hinder your comfort coming to me, I want to identify them right now—and hand them over to you ...

Oh God, when I think of how short life is—and how frail I am—it makes me feel ...

But when I think of how "the word of our God stands forever," I realize ...

Lord, when I really see you in all your power and greatness, even in the pain of my loss, I know ...

Lord, I remember you are the Good Shepherd and, even though I am in anguish, I am comforted because I know that you ...

Lord, I desire to share these "voices of comfort" from your Word by ...

Part Two

GOSPEL OF HOPE

Chapter 5

IN DEEPEST WATER AND DARKEST NIGHT

 MATTHEW 14:22–33

When you are beset by a storm and seemingly alone in deep waters and dark night, exhaustion and fears begin to assail the soul. But you are not as alone as you think, for you are in Jesus' heart and on his mind. There is hope, for he sees you and is coming for you … walking on the water.

A beautiful early spring day warmed the whole area and held the promise of a relaxing evening after work. Older school kids were energetically practicing their spring sports after school, and younger ones were happily playing in backyards and parks. I had left a bit early from work and on the way home picked up a pizza for the family. Like the day, our lives were pretty sunny, and for the most part we sailed along smoothly on calm waters. But a phone call I received when I returned home disturbed those calm waters. I was told to come to the hospital immediately, and as I hurriedly drove there, I sensed storm clouds gathering. A feeling of dark foreboding washed over me, and that feeling proved true when the chaplain broke the news that my daughter had died on the track field. The hurricane-force winds that hit my heart at that moment knocked me flat. The sunny day had turned into a dark personal maelstrom of misery and grief, threatening to sink my soul into a watery abyss.

In the terrible times following the loss of Rachel, I felt often that I was about to go under. I felt as if I had been struck broadside by the perfect storm, and the turbulent seas and strong winds threatened to swamp me and send me down for the last time. How would I survive, and who would rescue me now? In the midst of this dark night and deep waters, God brought hope to my broken heart, reaching out his hand of mercy to me through an unexpected corner of Scripture.

One of the great rescue stories in the Bible is the popular story of Jesus' miraculous walking on the water—an account given in three gospels (Matt. 14:22–33; Mark 6:45–52; John 6:16–24). Interestingly, all three place the well-known miracle story of Jesus feeding five thousand men (plus women and children) from the little child's lunch bag of five loaves and two small fish right before the story of his walking on the water. Without spiritualizing every detail in these stories, both miracle stories seize our attention and together demand that we fix our eyes firmly

NOTHING CAN PREVENT JESUS FROM COMING TO HIS FOLLOWERS. IN DARKEST NIGHT, OVER DEEPEST WATERS, AND THROUGH STORMY WINDS, HE APPROACHES THEM.

upon Jesus. He stands at the center of both. Therefore, these stories call us to search deeply, to ponder their profound spiritual disclosure about the person of Jesus. We are meant to see beyond the bread to the bread giver who said, "I am the bread of life" (John 6:35, 48–51). Likewise, the story of Jesus walking on the water demands that we peer past the miracle to the Master of the waves and the wind and the sea who announces his presence on the water by the disciples' boat with the suggestively succinct words, "It is I."

STRUGGLING AND STRESSED IN A STORMY NIGHT AT SEA

Part of the gospel story's depiction of Jesus, however, comes from the setting of the narrative. To understand what the gospel writers want us to see about Jesus requires an appreciation of certain key aspects of the story's setting and context.

Departure by Design

Remember that the disciples had just recently witnessed, and even taken a part in, a spectacular miracle as Jesus multiplied the five loaves and two little fish into more than enough food for thousands of people. I imagine they were dumbfounded by Jesus' demonstration of power as they finished picking up the twelve baskets of leftovers. Hanging out with Jesus now was the "in" thing for the crowds, but especially so for the disciples who were Jesus' intimate friends. He was the ultimate breadwinner, and no doubt they loved being closely associated with the great hero of the day.

What a change it must have been for them when soon afterward Jesus "made the disciples get into the boat and go on ahead of him to the other side" (Matt. 14:22). Leaving Jesus was not their idea; it was definitely his plan. The simple word "made" translates a very strong verb meaning that he "compelled" or "forced" them to do this. We are meant to notice Jesus' firm directive that put the disciples on their own, alone and separated from him for a time. They depart by Jesus' design, a key beginning note that imparts a pregnant sense of divine purpose to what follows. Who could miss the further important implication here that Jesus is Lord? He is in command and remains fully in control, sovereign over the situation, whatever might come. They go on then, alone and apart from Jesus, yet just as surely in the midst of the waters of his will.

Darkness and Deep Waters

So off the disciples went on their journey of several miles across the northern part of the Sea of Galilee. By sunset they were already a few miles out to sea, struggling mightily against a storm of hostile winds and high waves—not uncommon on this sea near mountains—buffeting their boat badly. Their struggle against the elements continued without relief, and after hours of straining at the oars, even these experienced fishermen were showing signs of stress and deep concern for their safety. The struggle continued unabated late into the dark night. Jesus finds them in this state at the "fourth watch of the night" (Matt.14:25; 3:00 a.m.–6:00 a.m.). After long hours of fighting the storm in the murky darkness, yet making little headway, weariness, fear, and stress undoubtedly began to seep into their souls. The Gospels paint a picture of them as feeling exhausted, drenched, alone, adrift, and downright scared.

In the days following our daughter's death, a trail of compassionate people visited our home, reaching out in a variety of kind, supportive ways. Churches extended themselves graciously to us with what services they could provide. Family members flew in from across the country and stayed to help us through those first difficult days. Then the funeral took place, and the graveside service ended. Inevitably the family members returned home, and the visits from friends and pastors tailed off to a bare trickle. After struggling to hold it together and fulfill responsibilities, physical and emotional exhaustion set in. I vividly recall terrible feelings of isolation. I felt adrift and buffeted by wave after wave of emotional seas, hour after hour and day after day. It wore us down. As if in the middle of a storm, blown by hostile winds and beaten up by the waves, we continued to strain at the oars of living—but it was taking a terrible toll on our souls. In a deeply personal way, I identify with the disciples' struggle in those deep waters on that dark night, a poignant symbol of my own struggle with overwhelming feelings of grief in the lonely aftermath of my daughter's death. We wondered whether we were going under, feeling isolated in the midst of a storm. We desperately needed rescue, but from where would it come?

Saved from Sinking

Students have wondered sometimes why Jesus would perform such a seemingly outrageous miracle like walking on the water. Aside from the obvious rescue result, was he just showing off? In a sense, of course, the answer is yes, for the Gospels clearly present Jesus as showing us something about himself—in what may be called an "epiphany" (manifestation) story. Revealed is a God who brings hope and strength to us when, like the disciples, we feel we're about to sink beneath it all.

Watchful Prayer and Care

After sending the disciples on ahead and dismissing the crowds, Jesus goes by himself up a mountainside to pray. In context it is understandable, since John the Baptist's disciples had just told Jesus that Herod had beheaded John (Matt. 14:12), Jesus' relative and great prophetic supporter. Undoubtedly, Jesus' heart was heavy after hearing such terrible news, and naturally he would have sought some time alone to grieve John's death and pray—likely also thinking of the path of suffering and death that loomed ahead for himself.

Further, since each gospel account of Jesus' walking on the water mentions his praying, that prayer must have been oriented in part to the disciples' experience in the storm. Jesus' prayer for his followers demonstrated his deep concern for them. To follow Jesus and his commands would require much hardship and struggle—a matter that called for serious conversation with the Father. Interestingly, Mark adds the detail that Jesus "*saw* the disciples" (Mark 6:48) and was aware of their struggle in the stormy seas—an incredible feat of vision itself at night from a distance during a storm. Though the disciples felt alone and apart from Jesus in the midst of deep waters on a dark night, they never ceased being in the Master's heart and hand. Though seemingly distant, for Jesus they were never out of mind or out of sight, neither forgotten nor abandoned. Soon, they, too, would know that.

Walks to Us with Power

Having seen them and recognizing their situation, Matthew tersely and simply says, "Jesus went out to them, walking on the lake" (14:25). This stunning miracle shows Jesus coming to them where they are, with supernatural power walking right over and through every natural barrier. Nothing can prevent Jesus from coming to his followers. In darkest night, over deepest waters, and through stormy winds, he approaches them. Nothing can separate them from his gracious advance. He will come.

Interestingly, Jesus comes at the end of the night (3:00 a.m.–6:00 a.m.), after they had already struggled against the elements for hours and were likely nearing the edge of panic. Why come then? Why wait? The text does not say, though we do well to remember at this point that Jesus had compelled them to go, that he was prayerfully watchful over them, and he was ready and willing to come to them. However mysterious his plans might appear, he had never removed his loving and guiding hand from their lives. Perhaps their struggle in the stormy waters represents the proverbial teachable moment, a situation when the disciples, in a time of desperate need, would pay special attention to what transpired and learn an irreplaceably critical lesson—a lesson about Jesus that, once learned, would give them indefatigable hope and a faith that would hold them steady in him through whatever life storms would come their way.

Words That Encourage, Strengthen, and Comfort

While the main matter in this story is the narrative of the events themselves, the words spoken by Jesus—and also Peter and the apostles—are of special importance. The dialogue reveals more clearly to us how to understand these miraculous events and so rightly apply them to ourselves.

WHEN OVERWHELMED BY HARDSHIP OR SUFFERING, WE NEED TO HEAR FOR OURSELVES JESUS' WORDS THAT ENCOURAGE US TO TAKE HEART AND BE FEARLESSLY AND CONFIDENTLY HOPEFUL.

The first response of the disciples when they saw Jesus coming to them—in the middle of the lake, in the dark, and walking on the water—was terror. Clearly they did not recognize him, and perhaps knowing the popular belief of that time that the seas were home to evil spirits, they feared that an apparition from the domain of the dead was coming for them. Given the stress of their situation, the terror they were already likely experiencing came to a head in this horrifying spectacle as they cried out in their terror, "It's a ghost" (Matt. 14:26). So fear was their first reaction, not faith.

Jesus, understanding their fear, immediately speaks to their troubled hearts: "Take courage! It is I. Don't be afraid" (Matt. 14:27). The calls to take heart and not be afraid are straightforward and needed, but most significantly Jesus' words of self-identification, "It is I," stand at the center of those two calls and give a core personal focus for persevering courage and hopeful confidence in the face of the storm. The focal point now is clearly on Jesus, the source of hope for them in this troubling situation.

WHEN WE FIND OURSELVES SINKING BENEATH WHATEVER DIFFICULTIES COME OUR WAY, JESUS THE GREAT LIFE SAVIOR STANDS READY AND ABLE TO STRETCH OUT HIS HAND AND LIFT US UP AGAIN.

"It is I" translates more literally "I am." Though at one level the phrase may mean a normal "It is I, Jesus," the miraculous context of the story itself strongly suggests that we should also hear in these words an intentional echo of the special personal name of God revealed to Moses in Exodus 3:14: "I AM has sent me [Moses] to you." God himself ("I AM") was present with Moses in bringing hope and freedom to his enslaved people. That Jesus uses such a theologically loaded phrase to identify himself in the midst of their hardship bears overtones of Jesus' divinity that must not be missed. Jesus reveals himself as the great "I AM"—the unique presence of God himself (see John 8:58), powerful for them in their trials. Earlier in the gospel, on another occasion, Jesus miraculously quieted stormy waves and seas (Matt. 8:27). His disciples gawked at him in the boat while wondering aloud: "What kind of man is this?" An answer to that question now grows clearer, for here the gospel reveals that in Jesus the almighty, powerful presence of God himself resides. Intriguingly, Job, in the midst of his terrible suffering, affirmed that God alone "treads on the waves of the sea" (Job 9:8). This story, therefore, further unveils the concealed majesty of Jesus in the announcement: "I am he."

When overwhelmed by hardship or suffering, we need to hear for ourselves Jesus' words that encourage us to take heart and be fearlessly and confidently hopeful. We must take to heart his words of comfort, words whose power resides in him who speaks them into our hearts and is himself the incarnate Word of God—Jesus, the very presence of God for us. The earliest Christian martyrs took this story as a pledge of Christ's aid, a promise of his saving presence to all who trust and obey him. And so it is still.

Following the death of our daughter, we received many good Christian books and other meaningful gifts to help us through our grief. We appreciated them deeply. I valued the insights of journey-of-grief books, counseling books, devotional books, and other kinds of writings. Nevertheless, at the end of the day I found that the Word of God— whether through good biblical preaching or my own reading—consistently tapped into my heart as nothing else could. Through the anointing of God's Holy Spirit, touching and teaching me afresh in the words of Scripture, I found myself comforted, healed, and renewed. In the biblical Word I encountered anew the living Word, Jesus, and rediscovered both joy and hope in the midst of my suffering.

Works to Save Us When Sinking

It is fitting that Matthew's gospel alone includes Peter's request to come on the water out to Jesus (14:28–31), since his gospel highlighted the varying responses of people to Jesus (see the preceding chapters in Matthew). Following Jesus' invitation to "come," Peter's bold walk begins well as he proceeds miraculously toward Jesus on the water, but when he sees the wind and the frightening surroundings, he no longer sees Jesus and begins to sink. Peter cries out to Jesus, "Lord, save me!" At once Jesus lifts Peter up, chides him by calling him "little faith," and questions why he ever doubted at all. Two matters draw attention in this little episode—one about Jesus and one about Peter.

Jesus does invite Peter to come to him, and it is undeniably Jesus who sustains Peter as he makes his way over the water to Jesus. That his power supports Peter is clear from what happens when Peter's eyes waver from Jesus to the wind and waves—he begins to sink. But what strikes me most is that when Peter cries out with the evocative words, "Lord, save me," Jesus the "Lord"—another loaded term pointing to Jesus' divinity for Matthew—reaches out instantly and saves him. Only then, when Peter is safely in his hands, does Jesus rebuke Peter for his small faith and doubt. So despite Peter's distracted doubt, Jesus grasps him firmly and places him safely in the boat. Jesus' gracious care for this impetuous and imperfect saint comforts my heart and calls for my greater trust in him.

IT SHOULD NOT SURPRISE US THAT PEOPLE WHO UNDERGO SEVERE TRIALS HAVE PERIODS WHEN DOUBT MIXES WITH TIMES OF PERSEVERANCE, FAITH, AND HOPE.

Peter intrigues us with his humanity. One moment his faith flies high, and he walks on water. The next moment a "strong wind" distracts his focus on Jesus and down he goes. Peter is a paradox, an example of both faith and doubt. In big faith Peter begins his walk, but soon he sinks and receives the humiliating title "little faith." Perhaps we like Peter so much because we identify with his inconsistency, with both his moments of great faith and his times of doubt. The story as a whole then appears to be a test of faith and spiritual growth, with Peter representing all the disciples. Matthew climactically focuses more on Peter's sinking than his success, and so the story of Peter here works mainly to call us to deeper trust in Christ precisely where the waters are deeper. We must remember that what looks like it is going to be over our heads is already under Jesus' feet. Most of all, when we find ourselves sinking beneath whatever difficulties come our way, Jesus the great life Savior stands ready and able to stretch out his hand and lift us up again.

Summoned to Worship

Call to Worship

When Jesus and Peter reach the boat, they climb in. Once Jesus is there, the wind ceases. One can only imagine the drenched disciples sitting dazed and amazed, no doubt feeling an eerie sense of déjà vu as they recalled an earlier boat excursion when Jesus had also miraculously quieted winds and waters (see Matt. 8:23–27). On that earlier occasion they responded with wonderment ("What kind of man is this?"), but here they go on to *worship* Jesus—recognizing that his transcendent power over the physical world meant something profound about his identity. This story calls us also to go past amazement to adoration, past wonderment to worship.

Confession of Faith

In their worship the disciples revealed their growing understanding of the magnificence of the person of Jesus: "Truly you are the *Son of God*" (Matt. 14:33). Admittedly, the disciples may not have fully understood all the implications of what that confession meant. The more negative ending to this story in Mark 6:52—"for they had not understood about the loaves; their hearts were hardened"—suggests the disciples' perception of Jesus' person was not yet matched by an understanding of what that position as Son of God meant for his care for them. Yet the more positive ending of Matthew and the more negative ending of Mark should be seen not as contradictory but as complementary and quite true to life for believers. Followers of Jesus regularly experience a mix of faith and doubt, combining stark moments of trust and understanding with times of wavering and obtuse ignorance. Matthew's emphasis, however, focuses on their worship of Jesus as the Son of God, a profound insight into the question of who Jesus is in relationship to God and to us. We should all build on that truth about the person of Jesus and heed this story's call to trust Jesus the Son of God more and more, especially in his providential care for us in the midst of our trials and sufferings.

It should not surprise us that people who undergo severe trials have periods when doubt mixes with times of perseverance, faith, and hope. Often, after the death of Rachel, when I experienced those disconcerting mixed feelings, I felt guilty because of my lack of faith. Not long ago, just days before a fellow professor died of cancer, she and I sat together one final time this side of glory as brother and sister in Christ. Knowing my own loss, she recognized a kindred spirit. We spoke openly together, sharing about the real spiritual struggles that so often accompany deep waters and dark nights. Quickly, though, guilt and anxiety receded into the background, and together we found ourselves "seeing" Jesus again, feeling his love and forgiveness wash over our souls. Together we looked forward to the full salvation only he can give. I admit my "little faith" and my wavering focus on Jesus, though I find his grace amazing and his forgiving hand lifting me up again and again. Ultimately, I always return to childlike trust in God, compelled over and again by the love of God for me shown in Christ Jesus. As Peter himself said soon after, when challenged by Jesus on whether or not he would continue to follow him: "Lord, to whom shall we go? You have the words of eternal life. We believe and know that you are the Holy One of God" (John 6:68–69). So, like Peter, I hold on firmly to Jesus the living Word and to the eternal Word of God that continues to speak out in Scripture.

The gospel of John's telling of this story ends in an interesting way. Jesus gets into the boat with them, and "immediately the boat reached the shore where they were heading" (6:21). Not only had Jesus walked to them on the water and stilled the seas, but he also brought them safely home. Such assurance of divine authority and protection is reminiscent of Psalm 107:23–32, which celebrates God's power over the wind and the waves as he brings sailors home safely to shore. Sometimes when I feel like a storm-tossed sailor, I take great comfort in the reality that Jesus will bring me, too, safely home.

Where Is the Hope?

The story of Jesus' walking on the water brings hope to our hearts, for there we see his watchful care, his ability and desire to come to us no matter where we are, his identity as one with God, and his divine authority to reach down in saving power and lift us up again. The only question, then, is whether or not we will entrust our lives to him, worshipping Jesus alone as the Son of God and Savior who gave his life for us on the cross. In Jesus, hope itself comes to us again and again— walking on the water.

"Here Is My Heart, Lord ..."

Lord, I need to talk with you about a storm in my own life where I've encountered a deep water and dark night kind of experience. It was when ...

I want to do your will, God, yet sometimes in difficult times it seems like no matter how hard I "row," I'm all alone and making no progress at all. Help me remember ...

Knowing that you prayed for the disciples and saw their struggles, Jesus, shows me that you ...

Lord, the fact that nothing can stop you from "walking on the water" to come to your followers encourages me because ...

Jesus, I need to hear your comforting words to the stressed-out disciples in the boat as words you also speak now to my own heart ...

... "Take courage" tells me ...

... "It is I" shows me ...

... "Don't be afraid" reminds me ...

Oh God, I really identify with Peter in his moment of great faith in the midst of stormy seas because I, too ...

... But I also identify with Peter, Lord, when he begins to sink, because like him I, too ...

Lord, I feel called even now to bow down before you. I worship you ...

Jesus, I know I'm not the only follower of yours in such a "boat," so give me opportunities to reach out to others using this great Bible story and tell them ...

Chapter 6

WHEN THERE IS NO SIGN OF LIFE

——⚜ JOHN 11:1–44 ⚜——

*Frustrated and confused, yet holding on to a strong faith
that believes things could and should have been different,
regretful "if-only" thoughts rise up and doubts creep in
unbidden. Can I yet hope and trust? Yes, I still believe …*

*I am the resurrection and the life. He who believes in me
will live, even though he dies.*

—JOHN 11:25

My face wet with sweat and tears, I bent over the cold hospital table
and held the still-warm face of Rachel. As her body grew cooler,
so did my spirit. My soul cried out within me with the overpowering
desire to breathe life back into her again. I poured out prayers, yet a
sense of powerlessness gradually crept over me. I collapsed in grief as a
sense of utter impotence overwhelmed me in body, soul, and spirit.

In that desperate moment I would have sacrificed anything for the
godlike power to give life. But I am not God. I could not breathe life
back into my daughter. As time passed, I discovered the truth that

when there is no sign of life, God graciously provides one for us in Jesus Christ.

One of the greatest stories told in the Gospels is an account in John where Jesus gives life to a dead man. John built into his gospel "signs"—miracles, in fact—that act like movie previews giving the observer suggestive glimpses of the bigger picture. John's signs each point to key parts of the bigger gospel picture of what God was doing in Jesus. John 20:31 says, "These [signs] are written that you may believe that Jesus is the Christ, the Son of God, and that by believing you may have life in his name."

The sixth of those signs unfolds in John 11 around the emotionally loaded event of the death of Jesus' close friend Lazarus—a stunning scene designed to call us to believe in this Jesus. Though stretched to the breaking point, we can still believe.

LIKE THE DISCIPLES, SOME OF LIFE'S DETOURS PUT US IN SITUATIONS WE WOULD RATHER NEVER FACE.

THE DISCIPLES

JESUS WORKS IN MY LIFE'S DELAYS AND DETOURS (JOHN 11:1–16)

Delays and Detours

How striking and surprising that Jesus would delay after the arrival of urgent news about Lazarus's critical condition. Surely he would rush to the side of his close friend and perform one of the healing miracles for which he had become famous. But Jesus delays two days (v. 6).

Then, after two days have passed, Jesus appears to change course and decides to go to Lazarus after all. Jesus' disciples are confused and openly wonder what he is doing. The disciples thought Jesus meant Lazarus was not fatally sick. Lazarus's hometown, as well, was in the area where Jesus' most violent enemies lived. When tragedy strikes, crushing our plans and hopes, life halts. Cruel twists in timing turn our worlds upside down. If only we had gone through that intersection thirty seconds earlier or later, things would have been so different. Like the disciples, some of life's detours put us in situations we would rather never face. Tension wells within us. Why are these things happening? We question whether God really knows what he is doing.

DELAYS AND DETOURS *STRETCH OUR FAITH* IN GOD.

Divine Design

Jesus himself points in two directions that tell something of what was going on in the divine design. First, he said it was to *show God's glory*, "so that God's Son may be glorified through it" (v. 4). For John, God's glory was revealed in Jesus himself, through his life, death, resurrection, and ascension. "God's glory" here does not refer to the praise of God but to God's action in Jesus. Through Jesus, God grants eternal life to all who believe in him. So Lazarus's death pointed to Jesus' death and glory. Not coincidentally, John 11 concludes with Jesus' enemies now seriously plotting to kill him, a plan they would successfully carry out. For John's gospel, as well, God's glory would be revealed in Jesus' resurrection.

The raising of Lazarus hinted at God's life-giving power, but that power was realized to its fullest eternal extent in the raising of Jesus and the promise of eternal life to all who believe in him. Here, then, is a delay immersed in much deeper spiritual waters. Though the disciples didn't understand at the time, the delay would point to something greater and even more glorious about Jesus: his death and resurrection.

PHYSICAL DEATH ONLY MEANS WE SEE JESUS AND KNOW HIM THAT MUCH BETTER.

Second, such delays and detours *stretch our faith* in God. Jesus actually says he was glad he delayed until after Lazarus died. He told his disciples that "for your sake I am glad I was not there, so that you may believe" (v. 15). Jesus had in mind his disciples' faith in him. This experience would stretch their trust in Jesus because even without their understanding, and in spite of truly dangerous circumstances, he was calling them to trust him and continue to go with him.

Thomas is the only disciple mentioned. His biting remark in verse 16 calling for the disciples all to go along with Jesus to death shows his faith stretched almost to the breaking point. It made no sense. It seemed the wrong thing to do. Wasn't Jesus making a terrible mistake here? But Thomas did go. However fearfully, he went. However much his attitude suffered, he still held on to Jesus and followed.

Life's delays can threaten to break our faith. In the midst of a torturous life detour, we may feel at the brink of unbelief. Does God really know what he is doing? This is obviously a mistake, isn't it? The loss of my daughter took me to the point where "God is so good" ceased being a happy children's chorus and became a statement of profoundest faith.

Like Thomas, my anxieties and fears bubbled to the surface. The lack of logical answers upset me. But like Thomas, I still trusted the Jesus who worked—and still works—in the heart-wrenching losses, delays, and detours of life.

I still believe in the Jesus who ...

JESUS WANTS US TO TRUST HIM FOR THE GREATEST GIFT OF ALL (JOHN 11:17–27)

Martha, one of Lazarus's sisters, comes onto the scene in the next section of the story. She goes out alone to meet Jesus before he gets to their home in Bethany.

If-Only Belief

Martha's first words to Jesus resonate with regret. "*If only* you were here, Jesus, you could've done something. You could've healed him; I know it." But Martha is not angry with Jesus. Instead, she still trusts Jesus and believes God will do whatever Jesus asks of him (v. 22). Martha's faith ran ahead of her understanding at this point, for what she said was truer than she knew. Jesus told her plainly that Lazarus would rise again, but Martha understood him to mean her brother would rise again on judgment day. She believed God Almighty could and would do that, but only Jesus could do something for Lazarus now. Only God has sovereign power over life and death.

I-Am Belief

Jesus' response to Martha resounds gloriously throughout the ages: "*I am* the resurrection and the life. He who believes in me will live, even though he dies; and whoever lives and believes in me will never die" (vv. 25–26). John stands alone among the Gospels in preserving so extensively the distinctive "I am" statements of Jesus. In the Old Testament, God reveals himself as "I AM," a self-descriptive phrase reserved for God alone. How stunning this must have sounded in Martha's Jewish ears to hear her friend Jesus say this! Jesus claims powers for himself that only God possesses—the power to raise the dead and give life itself. In Jesus himself, then, rest the supreme authority and sovereign power to give the greatest gift of all—eternal life.

We must be clear that Jesus was not promising that those who believe in him will not physically die, as his words "even though he dies" (v. 25) plainly teach. He does, however, mean that physical death is not the end of life for the one who believes in him. If death means separation, then at physical death we are separated from those we know in the physical realm. But Jesus told Martha those who believe in him "will never die" (v. 26), a further promise that at a spiritual level a believer will never be separated from God.

Physical death only means we see Jesus and know him that much better. Jesus raised Lazarus to make a point about himself and his omnipotent authority to grant life everlasting. Lazarus would die again physically, though he, like all true believers, would never be separated from Jesus.

JESUS UNFAILINGLY
REVEALS HIMSELF
AS THE SOURCE
OF TRUEST HOPE
AND COMFORT
AS HE OFFERS
THE PROMISE OF
EVERLASTING LIFE.

I-Do Belief

After Jesus' stunning statement, he pointedly asks Martha the central question of the New Testament: "Do you believe this?" (v. 26). Though she still did not fully understand the magnitude of his question or of her own answer—as the story goes on to show (v. 39)—Martha got her confession of Jesus perfectly right. "Yes, Lord, I do believe!" She elaborated a full-blown confession of Jesus as the Messiah, the Son of God, and as the biblically prophesied One who would come into the world. Martha offered no half-measure confession but a full personal acknowledgment of Jesus as her own Lord—with power to grant eternal life itself.

Like Martha, when personal loss strikes us, regrets may well cloud our spirits. But just as he did for Martha, Jesus unfailingly reveals himself as the source of truest hope and comfort as he offers the promise of everlasting life. Though we may not fully comprehend his promise, Jesus calls us once again to trust him and his life-giving power. With Martha, I still believe in Jesus.

I believe in the Jesus who ...

Mary

Jesus Walks with Us Personally through Our Grief (John 11:28–37)

In John's next scene, Mary, Lazarus's other sister, also comes out to meet Jesus. Though little is said between Mary and Jesus, he reveals his grief and shares the human feelings that inevitably surround such losses. Two emotional elements of the story stand out and demand a closer look: Jesus is both sad and mad.

The Sorrow of Jesus

Almost word for word, Mary's only recorded comment voices the same regret Martha first uttered: "Lord, if you had been here, my brother would not have died" (v. 32). Unlike the first, however, Mary's meeting with Jesus overflows with raw emotions of mourning and tearful sorrow.

Though Jesus says little to Mary, he is there for her. Rather than hollow, pet phrases, he offers instead his presence, unadorned and unfettered—a heartfelt presence, for Jesus shares her sorrow and cries openly with her (v. 35). Such a practice of presence calls for deep sensitivity and empathy. Our Great High Priest models such compassion to perfection as he walks with Mary and Martha through their loss.

Jesus' tears, however, beg a question. If Jesus knew that he was about to raise Lazarus and that they would share a meal later that day, why did he cry? Undeniably, Jesus grieved the loss, however temporary, of the relationship with his beloved friend. He grieved to see that same sense of loss in Mary and Martha. Jesus knew that humankind was created for relationship and that any severing of relationship causes agonizing sorrow.

Jesus also knew sin brought death—and the severing of relationships—into this world, and so he weeps over the separation death brings to the human experience. It was not meant to be this way. God created us for relationship with him and with his creation. Any disruption of such relational intimacy causes divine sorrow. But Jesus' emotions go beyond mournful sorrow.

The Anger of Jesus

Though English versions typically soften Jesus' emotion in 11:33 to being inwardly troubled or deeply moved, strong, convincing linguistic evidence on the meaning of the original word in Greek suggests John meant Jesus was angry. Though we might flinch from seeing Jesus' mourning colored with tones of deep anger, why should such emotion in Jesus surprise us? Those who have lost loved ones in tragic ways often wrestle long with deep-seated feelings of anger. But where is the anger directed?

I believe Jesus focuses his anger on sin and death and the consequent aloneness and separation it brings. Jesus seethes with anger as he confronts death and its destruction of divinely intended relationships.

In another gospel story (John 2:13–25) we find Jesus similarly angry when he sees corrupt religious leadership in the temple throwing up manmade barriers between people and their God. They had made the house of prayer and closeness to God into a den of thieves, robbing people not only of their money but also of a special opportunity to be intimate with God. Jesus was not just troubled; he was table-turning, whip-wielding angry. Anything that causes separation and loss of relationship calls forth Jesus' most powerful anger!

For those grieving a loved one, it liberates us emotionally to know that Jesus is not aloof from our loss, our pain, and our sense of anger. It liberates us further to see Jesus give full vent to his emotions. But it also instructs us to direct our emotions,

JESUS IS NOT ALOOF FROM OUR LOSS, OUR PAIN, AND OUR SENSE OF ANGER.

especially volatile ones like anger, accurately and appropriately.

Jesus knows our sorrows and shares our sense of anger—and he will do something about it.

I believe in the Jesus who ...

LAZARUS

JESUS WILL UNITE US AGAIN WITH LOVED ONES (JOHN 11:38–44)

When Jesus goes out to Lazarus's cave tomb, anger—the same word as used for Jesus' angry emotion as in verse 33—again engulfs his spirit (v. 38). I can almost feel Jesus' indignation at the stone sealing the tomb and separating him from Lazarus. Jesus bluntly commands: "Get that stone out of here!"

Grim Reality of Death

John leaves no room for doubt about the grim reality that Lazarus was dead. Denial remains a common feature of the grieving process, but here John permits no denial of Lazarus's death. His body had received the ceremonial Jewish wrapping treatment for dead bodies. He had already lain in the stony tomb sealed up four days. John, furthermore, includes in his account Martha's stark statement about the bad smell of Lazarus's body. Twice John bluntly refers to Lazarus simply as "the dead man." No, there remains no doubt, no possibility of denying this grim reality. Lazarus was dead.

Glorious Power of God

Despite Martha's objection, they finally remove the stone, and Jesus commands Lazarus—the "dead man"—with a loud voice of power and authority: "Come out!" Jesus is in complete control of the situation as he exercises God's glorious power to give life.

Imagine being there and seeing Lazarus ambling awkwardly from the mouth of the tomb, still hobbled by the grave wrappings on his body. Who could blame those gathered there for being dumbstruck? The pure shock—and likely, fear as well—immobilized them. Jesus has to direct them to move, telling them to unwrap Lazarus so he could move freely again.

The gospel writer permits no misunderstanding of the point of this miraculous sign. With Jesus' comment and prayer in 11:40–42, John ties everything back again to Jesus' focus on *God's glory* announced at the beginning of this story. To "see the glory of God" (v. 40) means to see the greater thing God was doing in the life of Jesus. Lazarus's death and raising points ahead to Jesus' death and resurrection, the "glory of God" through which God will bring life to everyone who believes in Jesus. We dare not miss the point. Jesus possesses *in himself* the sovereign authority and power to give life. "See me and believe in me," Jesus is saying, "and you are seeing the 'glory of God.' You, too, can inherit life forever-more through trusting in me. I am the resurrection and the life!"

As I sat dumbfounded and numb with shock in that emergency room, my denials rose up involuntarily. It had to be a bad dream. The moments took on a surrealistic feel. But when I entered the room where her still body lay, reality jolted me. My denials drifted softly away into sobs and silence. Rachel, whom I loved with every ounce of my being, was gone. That horrible reality sank into my whole being, and I felt crushed beneath the unbearable weight of separation.

Yet, something else remained in me that could not be denied. There could be no denying Jesus' power to give eternal life. Like never before, I grasped on to that hope. I knew Rachel had trusted Jesus with her life. She believed in him, and her life gave visible evidence of that reality; and because of that, I knew she was now safely in the hands of him who promised, "I am the resurrection and the life. He who believes in me will live, even though he dies; and whoever lives and believes in me will never die" (11:25–26).

I also believe that the sign of Lazarus and his loved ones' reunion points to Jesus performing a far greater reuniting of those who have believed in him. He will bring us back together again, to live with one another in his presence forever in heaven. Is it any wonder we who believe long to go home to heaven? It is our blessed hope!

Where Is the Hope?

When there is no sign of life, when death's reality separates us from our loved ones, then *God provides a sign of life*—a sign of life realized in Jesus himself. This passage shines like a beacon of hope to all who have experienced the heartbreaking loss of a loved one. God's Word here in John 11 also sounds out a clarion call to us to hold firmly onto faith in Jesus in the midst of such life-shattering experiences.

We can still believe in the Jesus who works even in life's disastrous delays and detours. We can still believe in the Jesus who wants to give us the greatest gift of all—eternal life. We can still believe in the Jesus who walks with us personally through our grief and who will unite us again one day with our loved ones.

Always, no matter what, we can still believe in Jesus.

"HERE IS MY HEART, LORD …"

Sometimes, Lord, the way things happen seems so confusing and frustrating that it stretches my faith almost to the breaking point. Why is it that …?

Because you, Jesus, are "the resurrection and the life," I …

Your anger at the death of Lazarus, Jesus, helps me focus my own anger at the death of my own loved one by …

Though I am suffering now the pains of separation and loss of personal touch with my loved one, your raising of Lazarus from the dead reminds me …

When you lead someone to me, Lord, who needs to hear this story of hope, give me grace and wisdom to point him or her especially to your …

Chapter 7

IN THE FACE OF DEATH

──❀ Matthew 26:36–46 ❀── (also Mark 14:32–42; Luke 22:40–46)

*Faced with his own suffering and death, Jesus breaks
down in a soul-wrenching prayer. He struggles in
confronting the agonizing pain of loss and separation, yet
his very struggle as he neared his own finish line of life
serves to show a pathway to enduring faith and hope.*

The last moments spent with a loved one before his or her death
often have a way of burning themselves into our memories, usually
with a sense of joy, but also sometimes with notes of great sadness and
regret. Especially with unexpected deaths, people in melancholic
moments often find themselves wishing they had done something more
or said something better or stayed a bit longer. I wish I had lingered
longer with my daughter that last morning as I dropped her off at
school. I wish I had hugged her more closely and said more than the typically brief farewell of "Love you; have a great day." It was the last time
… it could have been better.

Peter, James, John, and the other disciples vividly remember the last
time they were with Jesus before his crucifixion. Jesus had led them into

Gethsemane ("oil press" in Hebrew), a grove of olive trees near Jerusalem. There, he prayed. Knowing what pain lay ahead, he prayed with a turbulent intensity that starkly contrasted with the serene garden.

THE LOSS OF A LOVED ONE OFTEN USHERS IN A DANGEROUS TIME OF SPIRITUAL WARFARE.

Jesus had looked to his three closest friends—Peter, James, and John—for support, but they fell asleep repeatedly. They failed him. Worse yet, these drowsy disciples had just vowed that they would never let Jesus down and would always stand with him (Matt. 26:31–35). But by the next morning and the most infamous rooster crow of all time, Peter, the most adamant supporter among them, would three times deny that he even knew Jesus—a failure echoed by the disciples who fled and hid. This is the sad framework for the disciples' remembrance of their last time with Jesus. It was not their finest moment, and it definitely could have been better.

My five-year-old showed me her new WWJD bracelet recently and asked if I knew what the letters stood for. The What-Would-Jesus-Do letters are really as old as the Gospels themselves. They encapsulate a biblical call to seriously consider how to make our responses to life's joys and hardships match what Jesus would have done. Classic Christian writings like Thomas à Kempis's *The Imitation of Christ* and Charles Sheldon's *In His Steps* have expressed this call to Christlikeness for generations of believers. Yet, predictably, the Bible itself remains the best sourcebook of all for this call and demands our primary attention.

The story of Jesus' intense spiritual struggle in Gethsemane provides a poignant biblical model for facing great loss—even death itself—with enduring faithfulness and a heart of hope for the future. However dark the night, it was a shining moment for Jesus. It could *not* have been better. So, in answering the question "What did Jesus do?" we hear God's call to follow Jesus' example—to walk in his steps.

Seek the Support of Godly Friends

All the disciples were at Gethsemane (except Judas), but Jesus specially asked Peter, James, and John to come aside with him. Jesus bared his soul to them, confiding his deepest feelings: "My soul is overwhelmed with sorrow to the point of death" (Matt. 26:38). He reached out to them for support, asking them to *stay with him; watch and pray with him;* and, ultimately, *not to go astray from him.* However imperfect they were, Jesus still sought and valued the support of these godly friends.

Stay with Me

In asking them simply to "stay here with me," Jesus sought the simple support of their *presence* with him in his time of need. They did not need to say anything or perform some great ministry act, but just be there. Just staying with Jesus at that time was a concrete expression of their real love and the solid support he needed.

FACING THE REALITY OF DEATH WITH AN ALERTNESS AND DEPENDENCE ON FAITH IN GOD THROUGH PRAYER IS ABSOLUTELY CRITICAL.

Recently our pastor told the story of a little boy who had a wonderful relationship with an old grandfatherly neighbor. The two became good friends. One day the old man's wife passed away, and the little boy told his father that he was going over to see his elderly friend, so he did. Later, upon returning from his visit, his father asked the little boy what he had said to the old man. The little boy quietly replied: "Oh, I didn't say anything. I just helped him cry." What a beautiful picture of love— being emotionally present and personally available.

Watch and Pray with Me

Not only did Jesus desire the support of their presence (preferably conscious!), but he also wanted them to "watch": to be continually (literally, "be watching") alert, spiritually vigilant, and prayerfully engaged on his behalf. Jesus did not want to face that anguish alone and unsupported, and so he looked to his closest friends for such support. Interestingly, the term "watch" may also imply that Jesus asked them to act as sentries protecting his privacy so that he could pray as he desperately needed to pray. Confronting great sorrow and pain taxes the human soul to the limit, and, sometimes, appropriate protective measures may serve as invaluable support in such trying times.

Don't Go Astray from Me

Finally, Jesus' command to the disciples to pray (the verb's tense points to a continual spirit of prayer) focuses on a specific purpose: "so that you will not fall into temptation" (Matt. 26:41). Luke's gospel emphasizes both the dangerous time facing the disciples and their faithfulness to Jesus (twice giving the temptation warning: 22:40, 46). When the moment of truth arrives, will they be ready to stand with Jesus, or will they yield to the temptation to abandon him? To survive such trials they need to be truly troubled by the dangerous spiritual waters ahead and stay wakeful in a constant attitude of prayer. Sadly, in this case, their sleepy response points to their vulnerability to straying and stumbling— a stumbling to which they all too soon succumb. Though later forgiven, restored, and sent forth again by Jesus—they do finally learn the lesson (see Acts 4:24–31)! The disciples' sleeping here symbolizes what *not* to do when facing a crisis.

Jesus explains his warning with the famous words, "The spirit indeed is willing, but the flesh is weak" (Matt. 26:41 KJV). He points to a fundamental problem all humans must face. We often have a good intention plan (our human spirit wants to do the right thing) but suffer from a bad attention span (our flesh tends to drift off into spiritual sleepiness). This tension and gap between our desires and our deeds has troubled generations of committed believers. Our mortal human frailties (flesh) of body and mind will always beset us, and so we need help in doing the right thing. Prayer at its base means that I recognize my

THE JESUS OF THE GOSPELS DOES NOT SERENELY STAND APART FROM US, SUPERNATURAL AND SEPARATED, BUT IS ALMOST STUNNINGLY ONE WITH US IN OUR MOST BASIC HUMANITY, OUR FRAILTY AND MORTALITY.

need for God's help and that I choose to depend on him. Is it any wonder that Jesus calls us to pray and place ourselves wholly in God's gracious and powerful hands? On our own, we cannot stand.

The loss of a loved one often ushers in a dangerous time of spiritual warfare. Faith is severely tested. Such grievous loss frequently stresses relationships. Marriages, for instance, are often so stressed by the emotional turmoil of grief that they disintegrate. Satan, the destroyer, works overtime to destroy any relationships he can, leaving us yet more vulnerable to his malicious intents. Facing the reality of death with an alertness and dependence on faith in God through prayer is absolutely critical. When my wife and I turned our broken hearts over to God, our relationship became a point of strength instead of a bridgehead for Satan's attacks. Prayer enabled us to draw again and again upon the inexhaustible well of God's grace, pulling us closer to him and to each other.

Jesus valued relationships highly and craved the company and support of his dear friends, even though they would let him down. I remember the stream of people who reached out to us—relatives, friends, youth groups, churches, and even people who barely knew us. I don't know how we would have made it without the generous helping hands of so many when we were simply overwhelmed. Yet however much we valued their support, ultimately *there can be no substitute for seeking God himself,* and this is precisely what Jesus did (WWJD) in Gethsemane as he came face-to-face with suffering and death.

Share Your Heart Openly and Honestly with God

Totally Dependent on God

Ironically, while the three disciples lay down on the ground to snooze, Jesus also was on the ground—but in quite a different way. Jesus fell to his knees and then prostrated himself. Such a prayer posture was unusual. Standing and looking up was the norm for prayer. This extraordinary posture dramatically emphasizes Jesus' humility and desperate need of God in this time of great spiritual distress. He recognized that he was totally dependent on God—the indispensable starting point for effective prayer.

Traumatized to the Point of Death

Mel Gibson's movie portrayal of Jesus in *The Passion of the Christ* painted with painful vividness the physical and emotional stress Jesus underwent. Gibson's specific presentation of Jesus' prayer struggle in Gethsemane was no exception, as he dramatically captured the trauma Jesus experienced that night.

Jesus' prayer struggle in Gethsemane reveals his humanity with unvarnished honesty, not flinching from showing that he wrestled with the reality of suffering and death. The Jesus of the Gospels does not serenely stand apart from us, supernatural and separated, but is almost stunningly one with us in our most basic humanity, our frailty and mortality.

Without hesitation, Matthew describes Jesus' personal distress: "He began to be sorrowful and troubled" (26:37). These words emphatically underscore the intensity of his grief (*troubled* is better translated "deeply grieved" or "distressed"). Matthew then goes on to quote Jesus' own words: "My soul is overwhelmed with sorrow *to the point of death*" (v. 38). How remarkable to hear on Jesus' lips that within his own soul he was so distraught that it was "to the point of death"! It echoes the heartbroken psalmist who cried out: "Why are you downcast, O my soul? Why so disturbed within me?" (42:5, 11).

Luke's gospel particularly highlights the intensity of Jesus' internal struggle at the prospect of death looming before him. In an unforgettable image, the physician portrays Jesus' actual physiological reaction. In deepest anxiety Jesus perspires so profusely that it looked like drops of blood falling on the ground (22:44)—a portent of his crucifixion.

Together, the Gospels show Jesus nearly crushed with anguish and not hiding his brokenness and pain from God, nor even from his friends. I find Jesus' honesty and authenticity both challenging and encouraging. Like Jesus, I need not hide my emotions from God, as if having a downcast soul somehow offends heaven. Depression is a natural human response to great loss. Deep lowness of soul is not a sin, nor is there any guilt for grieving.† So God invites us to do as Jesus did—share openly and honestly our crushed hearts and souls with him. It is the indispensable starting point on the road to survival in hope.

SUBMIT YOURSELF TO
GOD'S SOVEREIGN WILL

However distressed Jesus was, he still found a way to express his heart's desires to God. Indeed, the gospel writers emphasize the content of Jesus' prayer. What Jesus says reveals much about his role as the Son of God and his relationship with God. Furthermore, Jesus' words also present a model for every believer to follow.

Drinking the Cup ... Dragging the Cross

For those Christians committed to the full divinity of Jesus, as I am, his thrice-repeated plea to God feels awkward: "My Father, if it is possible, may this cup be taken from me. Yet not as I will, but as you will" (Matt. 26:39). Nevertheless, Jesus' prayer request points us in hope-filled directions as we listen in anew to his conversation with God.

Relationship

Jesus begins by addressing God as "Father." Mark, in his gospel, puts together both the Aramaic and the Greek forms—"*Abba,* Father" (14:36). By calling God "Abba," Jesus grounds his request in his relationship with

---

† Please note that for "clinical" depression—chronic and continuous—one ought to see a professional counselor.

God. The word suggests a warm family closeness. For Jesus, God is not remote and disengaged from his life experience. Loving, trusting relationships are intimate. The heavenly Father, God, cares deeply for the Son, Jesus. Therefore, with confident hope and trust, Jesus appeals to that relationship as the starting point for everything he prays—"Abba, Father."

Remove This Cup

Jesus requested God to remove "*this cup*" from him (Matt. 26:39). In the New Testament the "cup" metaphor refers to Jesus' suffering and death. Yet Jesus also understood this to mean the Old Testament "cup of God's wrath," a metaphor for the terrible consequences of God's judgment upon sin. Though he knew he would suffer and die (Matt. 26:31; Luke 9:22), Jesus had no death wish. Here, in his real humanity, he naturally recoiled from the prospect of death and what it meant for him—sinless Jesus taking on himself all the evil and sins of humankind. Such an atoning death would bring forgiveness and reconciliation with God for all who would love and totally trust Jesus, *yet* such incredible loving sacrifice cost Jesus dearly. His identification with sinners and their sins on the cross meant separation from a pure and holy

THERE IS NO MORE PROFOUND HOPE THAN IN HAVING AN INTIMATE, LOVING RELATIONSHIP WITH THE LORD AND KNOWING HIM AS "ABBA, FATHER."

God. Though Jesus knew he would rise again (Matt. 26:32), his sense of impending alienation from God, a *loss of relationship* with his loving

Father God, explains Jesus' startling words on the cross: "My God, my God, why have you forsaken me?" (Matt. 27:46).

When a loved one dies, a sense of separation and aloneness assaults our souls—the agony of losing a treasured relationship of love. Memories of our times with our loved ones bring waves of loneliness and an acute sense of separation. Is it any wonder Jesus asked God what he did? No one wants to experience such pain. Yet, such is the measure of Jesus' sacrificial love for us all. For on the cross Jesus embraced that cup—and he drank it in our place.

Relationship Restored

Through the "cup," through the forsakenness of Jesus on the cross for our sins in the miracle of salvation, comes forgiveness and acceptance into the family of God for all who trust in Jesus—our own restoration. Like Jesus we may now address almighty God as "Abba, Father." There is no more profound hope than in having an intimate, loving relationship with the Lord and knowing him as "Abba, Father." This means we will never, ever truly be alone or abandoned. For believers in Jesus, physical death may still bring separation from loved ones, but only for a while. True relationship with God is unbreakable. It goes on forever in heaven in his presence, where we will be united again as family with all those who have loved Jesus and placed their lives in the hands of the loving Father.

Dedicated Most of All to God's Desires, Not Mine

Finally, we need to see that Jesus frames his request with words showing that what he wants most is God's will: "Father, if you are willing … yet not my will, but yours be done" (Luke 22:42). However much he might humanly desire another possible solution to the problem of human sin, as an obedient son he desires his Father's will most and fully intends to do it. "Not my will, but yours be done."

Someone might think of such submitting to God's will as a sort of fatalism or that Jesus' divinity makes his obedience utterly different from ours. But that is not the picture in the biblical story of Gethsemane. There the gospel writers emphatically depict Jesus' humanness at virtually every level. As the author of Hebrews says, in a passage that may well have Gethsemane in mind, "During the days of Jesus' life on earth, he offered up prayers and petitions with loud cries and tears to the one who could save him from death, and he was heard because of his *reverent submission*. Although he was a son, he *learned obedience from what he suffered*" (5:7–8). Like Jesus, when we humbly submit ourselves to God's will, trusting in his sovereign, fatherly heart, our prayers are valued and heard by God. Like Jesus, we learn obedience through the painful experiences of life, trusting in God through the hurt and finding his grace sufficient to see us through.

GOING FORWARD THROUGH GRIEF, SUFFERING, AND LOSS DEMANDS OUR GREATEST FAITH AND LOVE.

Jesus openly sought God for another pathway—but left no doubt that his primary desire was God's desire. Everything else was secondary. Such a spirit of submission challenges the soul of everyone who has ever experienced the painful death of a close loved one. Like Jesus, we feel conflicted spiritually when confronted by death. The sense of separation and loss of relationship cut deeply, and we naturally recoil. This tests our faith, for in the face of death, submission to Father God—placing all that we are in his loving hands—requires total trust. Thankfully, that trust is grounded in God's sovereign and loving will that our relationship with him be unending and unbreakable, an assurance powerfully given in Jesus' cross and resurrection.

Strength to Get Up and Go Forward

God's Gracious Help

Luke's gospel (22:43) alone gives us the detail that while Jesus was in Gethsemane "an angel from heaven" came to him and strengthened him. What a beautiful picture of God graciously reaching out to help someone sold out in faith to his will. The angelic aid shows God's desire to stand with his own in terrible times. They will not suffer alone, for he comes to them. Through his angel, God upholds Jesus with the strength to face the coming ordeal. However invisible such angelic divine aid might be in our own experiences, I believe that God does reach out in supernatural ways to help us face ordeals of suffering with strength beyond our own, standing with us who have taken a stand for him.

Going Forward from Here

The Gethsemane story closes with Jesus returning a third time to the three drowsy disciples, waking them up, and announcing that the "hour" (of Jesus' passion) had come for his betrayal by Judas into the hands of his enemies (Matt. 26:45). The disciples had failed badly as supportive sentries and prayer warriors, yet Jesus still calls them now to go forward with him to meet the enemy. He commands them simply, "Rise, let us go!" That last call— "let us go" (v. 46)—was used in armies as a command to advance into battle ("forward march!"). Jesus resolves to do God's will, and now he does not turn in flight but marches forward into battle—on to an ultimate victory, though at a terrible cost of suffering to himself.

On 9/11, terrorists commandeered a passenger airliner over the northeastern states of the United States. A handful of heroic passengers determined to take on the terrorists and stop their deadly plans. Todd Beamer is known to have called out to his fellow heroes: "Let's roll!" Advancing into the face of almost certain death, they managed to cause enough havoc with the terrorists that they thwarted the enemies' murderous goal of crashing the plane into a building full of people. Who knows how many thousands of people owe their lives to these men who went forward into harm's way?

Going forward through grief, suffering, and loss demands our greatest faith and love. Jesus marched forward into battle, full to the brim with love and faith. Thwarting the designs of the Devil to make death the last word on the battlefield for people's souls, Jesus turns the tables by turning his own suffering and death into the very means of life for myriad people who give their lives to him. In the midst of our own pain, our hurt, and our losses, Jesus still comes to us (sometimes waking us up!) with his call to go on, to go forward with him through the battles we must yet face in a world still afflicted by heartbreaking pain. We do not go on alone. He has gone this way before us, and now he will go forward with us.

Where Is the Hope?

When faced in Gethsemane with suffering and death, what did Jesus do? Following Jesus' example as he neared the finish line will put us on the same pathway to enduring faithfulness to God and a hope that strengthens us to go forward. So what did he do? Jesus looked for hope in friends (however imperfect) who shared his same devotion to God. He openly shared his broken heart with God, crying out in prayerful dependence on him. Jesus rooted his hope in his relationship with God as his (Abba) Father, whose loving will he trusted and desired absolutely and above all. Finally, the angelic aid Jesus received tells us there is hope in knowing that God has not abandoned us but reaches out to his own, giving strength to go forward through whatever may come.

"HERE IS MY HEART, LORD ..."

God, when I think about the "last time" I was with _____ I feel ...

*For a variety of reasons, it is hard for me to seek out others for support.
But I know godly friends could help, so help me ...*

*Jesus, all too often I'm like those sleepy disciples and not much use to others
who could use my support. I want to be more helpful, so ...*

*I feel like my loss has put me in the middle of a spiritual battlefield, Lord.
I really find my faith tested especially ...*

*God, knowing you are my "Abba, Father" reminds me in the midst of my
most difficult times that you ...*

*Lord Jesus, just remembering times together with _____ makes the loss
of that relationship almost unbearable, especially when ...*

God, submitting my desires to yours really challenges my faith because ...

*Knowing that you, Lord Jesus, "learned obedience through suffering"
reminds me that when I face hardship and suffering, I, too ...*

Chapter 8

AFTER THE DISASTER ... OPENING YOUR EYES AGAIN

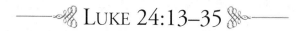 LUKE 24:13–35

Trudging along sadly on a road away from Jerusalem after Jesus' crucifixion, two little-known disciples of Jesus find their melancholic conversation interrupted by a stranger. His questions and sharing of Scripture with them strangely warmed their hearts, reigniting the dimming embers of hope within them. Could it really be? Was Jesus really alive? Later, as Jesus, whose body was broken for them, now broke bread in a meal with them, their eyes were opened ... to "see" Jesus again.

When I experience migraine headaches, the blinding pain so consumes me that I don't want to move, hear any sound, or even open my eyes until it subsides. For a time the world fades into the background as my pain totally preoccupies me. Only later do I open my eyes again.

A couple of days after Rachel died, I found myself wandering through a local grocery store as if in a cloud. Immediate family members had arrived, and I had to leave the cocoon of our home to get more food and some everyday household items. I well remember how strange that routine trip to the store felt. I was almost numb, and the world seemed drained of its color by a mist of grayness. Sounds were oddly muted, and I felt awkwardly foreign walking on even such familiar ground. I was so out of it that, I was later told, I walked right past people I knew without seeming to see them at all. I'd been blinded by the intensity of my emotional "migraine heartache." Only later was I able to open my eyes again.

JESUS LONGS TO GIVE US GRACIOUS HELP IN HIS PRESENCE, HIS WORD, HIS FELLOWSHIP, AND HIS PEOPLE PRECISELY IN THAT TIME OF OVERWHELMING PAIN.

In the last chapter of Luke's gospel (24:13–35), we find an exquisite little story of dashed hopes and rediscovered faith on the first Easter Sunday. Luke dramatically recounts the experience of two little-known disciples (Cleopas and an unnamed person) on the third day after Jesus' death. After the disaster of the crucifixion, they departed with deep sadness and confusion from Jerusalem and walked together on a road to the nearby town of Emmaus just seven miles away. Unrecognized by them, the risen Jesus—his body somehow "different"—joins and interacts with them on the journey. Moved by their time with him, at Emmaus they insist the stranger (Jesus) stay with them, and as they eat together their eyes are opened to recognize Jesus—who then disappears. At once, they return to the believers in Jerusalem to report their experience, adding their testimony to that of others that Jesus was truly alive. "He is risen indeed!"

Is it possible that after a disastrous loss, our hearts too can become so downcast and our eyes so clouded by our disappointment and dashed hopes that we can be spiritually blinded to the grace God wants to give us? Can our pain so preoccupy us that we cannot perceive anything else? When we mourn the loss of a deeply loved one, our hurt can so consume us that our eyes are closed to the very help we so desperately need—a help right next to us. Jesus longs to give us that gracious help in his presence, his Word, his fellowship, and his people precisely in that time of overwhelming pain. Will we open our eyes again ... and really see him right next to us?

WALKING ALONGSIDE US (LUKE 24:13–24) ... LOOK CLOSER!

Draws Them Out ... Listening

Jesus joined the two disciples as they were discussing the tragic events of the past couple of days in Jerusalem. He asked them about the events they discussed. Though he himself was the object of their discussion, Jesus drew them out with a simple, open-ended question (24:19): "What things?" How ironic that Jesus, of all people, would ask such a question and

JESUS, THE MASTER LISTENER, GRACES US WITH HIS OWN EARS READY TO HEAR AND TO HEAL US AFTER DISASTER HAS LAID US LOW.

then quietly and patiently listen while they tell him what had happened and how they felt about it. Such listening is a profound measure of his loving care for them.

We need to learn from Jesus. His wisdom and love are vividly demonstrated as he offers the two distraught disciples an opportunity to share and then carefully listens. What a comfort to know that Jesus, the master listener, graces us with his own ears ready to hear and to heal us after disaster has laid us low. Though they, like so many who experience great loss, wanted to draw away—as their literal withdrawal from believers in Jerusalem to Emmaus may symbolize—Jesus comes to them, walks alongside them, and wisely draws them out.

Disappointment

Luke concisely but dramatically presents the initial response of the two men to Jesus' question: "They stood still, their faces downcast" (24:17). Luke's term stresses their sad and despondent mood. Jesus' question takes them off guard, stopping them in their tracks, partly because they are shocked someone coming from Jerusalem wouldn't know about this, but also, I suspect, because they had to talk again about their loss and broken hearts. Discussing it again would not have been easy. Those struggling with the loss of a loved one can identify with not only their "downcast" faces but also their being caught off guard by unexpected (and seemingly ignorant) questions about the one we so recently lost. Responding can be painful as it dredges up emotional freight once again.

Their expansive response (vv. 19–24) shows they had tied high hopes to Jesus. They saw him as a mighty prophet in word and deed; and, what is more, they believed he would free ("redeem") Israel from oppressive powers and begin a wonderful time of God's own rule among them (the kingdom of God). His crucifixion, they thought, had cruelly dashed all such hopes and dreams. The sense of tragedy had been further heightened that very morning by the inexplicable and distressing disappearance of his body from the tomb.

Discernment Deficit

Their recounting of the mysterious absence of Jesus' body ends emphatically: "But *him* they did not see" (24:24). Here Luke employs irony once again. While they are retelling the story from that very morning when several Jerusalem disciples found only an empty tomb and did not see Jesus, Jesus himself is walking right alongside them—but *him* the two disciples now also did not see!

Luke puts the disciples' puzzling inability to recognize Jesus (their discernment deficit) in an intriguing light: "But they *were kept from* recognizing him" (v. 16). In the gospel accounts of Jesus' postresurrection appearances, he looked different somehow, not always immediately recognizable (a "different form" [Mark 16:12]). It is also true that their broken hearts hindered their abilities to see well. Yet here Luke now accents the fact that they *"were kept from"* recognizing Jesus. Likely this means that God himself concealed Jesus' identity for a time—a divinely designed concealment. (In Luke 9:45 and 18:34 a similar "hidden" theme also occurs.) But why would God so conceal Jesus' identity from them? I believe that God, in his sovereign wisdom, knew they needed to be prepared to "see" Jesus as the risen Lord in the right light, readied for the unexpected revelation that the crucified Jesus is now walking around alive.

WORD OPENED TO US (LUKE 24:25–27) ... LISTEN MORE CAREFULLY!

Having patiently listened to them and having allowed them to express their broken hearts, Jesus continues a process of opening their eyes, so they could "see" again. He does this by taking them back to the Scriptures, teaching them there the full truth of the Bible concerning himself as the Messiah (Christ) who, in God's gracious and sovereign plan of salvation, *had to* suffer to atone for people's sins and only then be raised up in glory ... raising up believers to new and eternal life.

Fuller Understanding of Jesus

Jesus gets their attention first of all by lovingly and firmly chastising them (24:25) for not listening more carefully (and more fully) to what God's Word really said. Indeed, in his brief, summarizing look at what Jesus said to the two disciples on the road, Luke emphatically stresses that Jesus taught them *all* the Bible said about himself (focused on the dominant theme given in verse 26). Repeatedly, Luke goes out of his way to say Jesus explored the Scriptures in a full and complete way—note that *all* occurs three times in verses 25–27. Such fuller biblical teaching was critical, Jesus recognized, in helping them understand God's work in himself as Messiah. Their truncated understanding of the Scriptures had left them troubled, uncertain, without hope ... unable to "see."

WE SHOULD LISTEN CAREFULLY TO OUR HEARTS, ESPECIALLY WHEN OUR SENSES CONFIRM CLEAR BIBLICAL TRUTHS AND DRAW US CLOSER TO THE LORD.

Jesus' loving rebuke of the two disciples (v. 25) reminds me of something John G. Mitchell, the founder of Multnomah School of the Bible in Portland, Oregon, was fondly remembered for saying: "Don't you folks ever read your Bibles?" There was a chastising "edge" to the comment, but the loving intent was to urge people to pursue a fuller and better understanding of God's Word. In times of great loss, more than ever, we need to delve deeply into the Scriptures, where we may find our eyes opened again and be able to "see" God's sufficient grace.

Too many believers ignore the Bible, and it is therefore sadly silent in their painful experiences. Some are aware of bits and pieces of Scripture, but even then are curiously disconnected from their fuller biblical context. Often the Bible is experienced one verse at a time from here and there. Other times Scripture is used merely as a source of illustrations. Such a piecemeal approach does not allow God's Spirit to teach us fully from the Word. In this passage I hear a call to listen more carefully and more fully to what God's Word says—to listen longer to *all* that the Scriptures have to say. When we do, the fuller scope of biblical teaching comes alive and touches us precisely at our point of need.

At the close of Paul's third missionary journey he tells the dearly loved leaders of the church in Ephesus that he would never see them again. They were understandably grieved and wept openly over him as they said good-bye for the last time. After giving necessary directions and encouragement, through his tears Paul sees the significance of reminding them, "I have not hesitated to proclaim to you the whole will of God" (Acts 20:27). Paul understood the vital necessity of knowing the truth of God *fully*, for only then can the Lord be "seen" in a way that brings persevering hope, lasting faith, and unfailing love.

Find Help in Understanding

Perhaps we should not be too hard on these two disciples here, since none of the other disciples, who were far closer to Jesus, were on track either at this point! Notably, Luke says Jesus explained the Scriptures to them at length (v. 27). Later in Jerusalem, in Luke 24:44–47, Jesus likewise had to take the time to bring even his closest disciples up to biblical speed, showing them that "everything must be fulfilled that is written about me." Jesus then marched them through the entire Bible front to back (v. 44). Luke then, interestingly, says, "He opened their minds so they could understand the Scriptures" (v. 45).

If disciples in Jesus' day who had actually been with Jesus himself needed help in understanding what the Bible taught, it should not surprise us that we also need someone who can come alongside us and help build into our lives a fuller understanding of God's Word and his ways. Indeed, we should seek out such sound teachers and value them greatly at all times, but especially when hard times are taking their toll on our souls.

WARM BREAD, WARMED HEARTS (LUKE 24:28–32) ... LINGER LONGER!

Invitation to Stay for Dinner

The two Emmaus disciples valued Jesus' teaching so greatly that when they finally arrived at Emmaus and Jesus was going to go farther, they insisted he stay for a meal so that they could continue their conversation. Interestingly, Jesus did not force his presence on them but awaited their invitation to him. With a sense of real urgency, they seized the opportunity to linger longer with Jesus, anxious to take advantage of a superb learning environment—a meal.

Lingering at length over a meal can cultivate intimacy in a relationship. The relaxed setting encourages deeper sharing about significant life issues. Then as now, a meal offers a great situation for listening, learning, and sharing life together. I remember not long after our daughter passed away that Larry and Ellen, two friends of ours, invited us for a meal. They knew our pain was quite fresh, but it did not scare them off. They were determined to offer themselves to us in ministry over a meal. The evening was seasoned with tears as we made our way through the various courses, though clearly the main course was healing. No doubt Jesus had joined us as we broke bread together over our broken hearts.

Inward Insight into Jesus

Now Luke begins to bring his story to a climax by telling how they honored Jesus by asking him to pray for the meal, giving thanks to God for the provision of their daily bread. Something struck the two disciples as distinctly familiar about the way Jesus broke the bread, prayed for the meal, and handed out the pieces. As Luke climactically reports, "Then their eyes were opened and they recognized him" (v. 31). At that recognition, when his ministry for that moment had been accomplished, Jesus disappears, putting the ball in their court. They now know the truth. His abrupt absence portends his soon-to-come ascension back to the Father, where he will remain unseen until the second coming. How will they respond?

First of all, as they look back (v. 32), they realize the earlier warmth of heart they felt—"our hearts burning within us"—had sprung from the presence of Jesus while walking with them on the road, then as he explained the Scriptures to them, and now, finally, as he broke bread for them in a thanksgiving prayer. We should listen carefully to our hearts, especially when our senses confirm clear biblical truths and draw us closer to the Lord. For the two disciples there was no longer any doubt. Scripture had actually taught it! Now, finally, their eyes are fully opened ... and they can "see." He really is risen from the dead. Jesus is alive, and in him there is hope for new life for all who trust him.

Around twenty-five years ago, my wife, my infant son, and I were snooping around the older parts of London, England, when we turned up a narrow street—Aldersgate Street. There, in a hall on May 24, 1738, a Bible study group had met and read together some of Martin Luther's work on the New Testament book of Romans. John Wesley went ("unwillingly," as his journal puts it) and listened. Later in his journal, Wesley penned the famous words so reminiscent of Luke 24:32: "While he was describing the change which God works in the heart through faith in Christ, *I felt my heart strangely warmed.* I felt I did trust in Christ, Christ alone, for my salvation; and an assurance was given me that he had taken my sins away, even mine."[1] That critical conversion event in Wesley's life, that burning inward insight into Jesus' person and work, ignited the flames of new life and hope in John Wesley ... and in the lives of thousands more in that century's great evangelical revival movement. The fires of faith still burn in every heart that "sees" in the risen Lord Jesus Christ alone the only true hope for life everlasting.

WITNESS WITH OTHERS TO NEW LIFE IN CHRIST (LUKE 24:33–35) ... LAUNCH OUT TOGETHER!

Sense of Urgency to Be with Other Believers

The two disciples who had previously walked away from fellow believers in Jerusalem now could not get back there fast enough. The text literally says at "the same hour" (v. 33 KJV) they got up and returned to Jerusalem. Though the sun was already setting, they dropped everything and with a deep sense of urgency left Emmaus immediately, spurred on by their experience with the risen Jesus. What a turnabout! This story began with a picture of these two disciples sensing such hopelessness that it caused them to walk away from the fellowship of believers. Now, in stark contrast, their rediscovered hope in Jesus and new life in him drove them back into community, to the fellowship of believers.

At church that Sunday morning I expected a fairly standard service, with some predictable promotion from the pastor to join a small group in our church. What I did not expect was what happened next. The pastor stepped aside, and a young couple took the podium. Together they shared their general Christian experience. They had been people of faith but inconsistent and not very connected to other believers. They told how the birth of their first son filled them with joy. Little James was the happy center of their lives. Then one day he became ill, and when things got worse rather than better, they took him to the hospital. The totally unexpected health problem was far worse than expected, and after a time of struggle, little two-year-old James passed away. Not surprisingly, their story hit home hard with me as I tearfully identified with their loss of a child. The couple went on to tell how, in their time of grief, they turned to the fellowship of believers with a renewed sense of urgency. They connected to smaller circles of people in the church and found the help and support they desperately needed through fellow believers living in real community. Heavenly hope in Christ has an earthly home for now, among the fellowship of believers in him ... where we can find the support we need to be able to open our eyes again and see Jesus.

Standing Strong Together in Witness

When the two disciples arrived where the Jerusalem believers were gathered, they were greeted by the confirming testimony of others: "The Lord is risen indeed" (v. 34 KJV). By this time, Peter himself also had seen Jesus. The two disciples added their witness to the others, explaining how they also had recognized Jesus. No doubt their shared testimonies strengthened each other and all who heard.

JESUS COMES AND — SOMETIMES EVEN UNRECOGNIZED BY US — OPENS OUR EYES AGAIN TO HIS LIFE-GIVING POWER.

Knowing human weakness and the need to confirm beyond all doubt that he was really alive, Jesus then once more reappears in their midst (vv. 36–43), demonstrating his resurrected body by offering up his hands and feet as evidence. He tops it off by eating a piece of broiled fish! As was the pattern with the two disciples on the Emmaus road earlier, Jesus once again opens the Word of God to this larger audience of witnesses, so they, too, could fully "see."

Luke concludes his gospel with this "witness" theme: "You are *witnesses of these things*" (v. 48). By no accident, Luke continues with this same theme at the beginning of Acts (volume two of Luke's two-part work) in that book's thematic verse: "You will be my witnesses in Jerusalem, and in all Judea and Samaria, and to the ends of the earth" (1:8). The eyewitness testimonies of the first disciples to the resurrection of Jesus gave them an unshakable conviction that his resurrection meant new life for all who would trust in him. As Luke's Acts of the Apostles goes on to show, these earliest disciples would bear (at great cost) the good news of Jesus' resurrection wherever they went … even to the ends of the earth.

Where Is the Hope?

The apostle Paul, whose "witness" dominates the book of Acts, wrote to some Asian believers that God chose to reveal a "mystery, which is Christ in you, the *hope of glory*" (Col. 1:27). Hope for now and for the future is wrapped up in relationship with Jesus, whose resurrection carries the assurance of new life for all who, by faith, invite Christ to dwell in their hearts. That is where hope ultimately resides—in Jesus.

The loss of a loved one can hurt so badly that we just want to shut our eyes and get away from it all. But, as the two disciples on the road to Emmaus discovered, hope is alive because Jesus is alive. Jesus comes and—sometimes even unrecognized by us—opens our eyes again to his life-giving power. He does this by opening our minds anew to his Word. How easy to forget God's Word in the throes of grief and loss. But that would be the greatest tragedy, for to close our eyes to the Scriptures is to close our eyes to Jesus … and to hope. But when we invite Jesus to stay with us, he who called himself the "bread of life" (John 6:35) shares his own life with us, and by faith we may now "see" in Jesus the very hope of glory itself. Only God's Word can reignite our hearts with hope. May the recognition of the two Emmaus disciples be ours as well: "Were not our hearts burning within us while he talked with us on the road and opened the Scriptures to us?"

"Here Is My Heart, Lord ..."

Lord, my loss sometimes feels like a "migraine heartache," especially when ...

To know that you patiently listen to me, even when I'm down in heart, frustrated, and confused like the two Emmaus disciples, means a lot to me, Jesus, because I know you ...

Lord Jesus, it is hard to "see straight" when my hurt so preoccupies me, like when ...

God, I believe you can open my eyes to see again through your Word, like you did with your two disciples, so please help me ...

Jesus, I know that too often I've held you off at arm's length, so when I see how the two Emmaus disciples urged you to stay with them longer ...

I recognize, God, that tying back into closer friendship with other believers will really help me, so ...

Lord, the costly witness of the earliest disciples inspires me. Give me opportunities to share my own witness of your touch in my own life with ...

... Help me to share from this story how you ...

Part Three

LETTERS OF HOPE

Chapter 9

GRIEVING AS THOSE WHO HAVE HOPE

————❦ 1 THESSALONIANS 4:13—5:11 ❧————

Unsure about the future, wondering about loved ones who have died, and uncertain about what to do now, anxiety rises. The truth of Jesus' second coming reaches down deep and touches my troubled heart with words of both comfort and challenge: "Therefore encourage each other with these words ... "

And so we will be with the Lord forever.

—1 THESSALONIANS 4:17

What happens to us when we die?

Throughout human history, we have contemplated this question with enduring curiosity. The answers vary wildly, from total denial of life after death to people who, after near-death experiences, testify to their glimpses of the afterworld.

The creator of Sherlock Holmes, Sir Arthur Conan Doyle, would seem a prime candidate for skepticism, yet personal loss drove him in his day to seek out mediums and spiritualists to speak again with the dead.

The first emperor of China reputedly recreated a miniature version of the world beneath his funeral pyramid, ensuring luxury and success for himself in the next world as well. The incredible archaeological find near Xian of a vast army of life-size terra-cotta soldiers testifies to the seriousness of this expectation.

Contemporary popular culture, as seen especially in movies like Robin Williams' *What Dreams May Come* or Bruce Willis's *The Sixth Sense*, has shown keen interest in the afterlife and ways in which it (often supernaturally) touches our existence here.

The point is clear: Humanity is insatiably curious and speculative about what happens after death.

Awash in an unsettling sea of human speculation, we must ask what God's Word says. What guidance does the Bible give, and how does it impact our lives as we grieve over loved ones who have died?

In our home's entryway is a small collection of memorial items for Rachel. Displayed there are pictures, memorable personal items, and, at the center of the grouping, a lovely piece of calligraphy artwork given to us by an artistic Christian friend containing the words of 1 Thessalonians 4:14–17. The climactic words, "and so we will be with the Lord forever" (v. 17), point us to the very substance of our hope as Christians—our "blessed hope" (Titus 2:13) in the return of Christ, who will bring about the greatest family reunion of all time in a home that will endure forever. That message of hope inspires us daily to endure and look forward with anticipation to being together again with Rachel. Our relationship has not ended. It has only been interrupted for a time, and we will be reunited once more forever at the second coming of Christ.

Paul addresses this great future vision of hope in a broader passage of his first letter to the Thessalonians (4:13—5:11), to a group of new believers whose time under his teaching was cut short by persecution (see Acts 17:1–9). This interruption left gaps in the Thessalonians' understanding of Paul's gospel teaching about the destiny of deceased Christians and the relationship to the second coming of Christ. Their grief over the untimely deaths of beloved fellow believers had left them anxious, distressed, and unsure about the future. Many today still identify with that kind of unrest of the soul, grieving the loss of loved ones with anxiety and uncertainty.

Paul responds in a twofold way, each part similarly and emphatically concluded by a call to "encourage each another" (1 Thess. 4:11; 5:11) with the very truths he was now sharing with them. To those struggling with grief and loss, Paul's exhortation to mutual encouragement envisions a different kind of grief, a grief indelibly colored by a hope-filled encouragement—an encouragement that inspires both comfort and challenge.

COMFORT: GETTING TOGETHER AGAIN (1 THESS. 4:13–18)

The Thessalonians' uncertainty about the destiny of their deceased loved ones caused them to grieve in a hopeless way that Paul saw as inappropriate to their Christian faith. To grieve with "no hope," as Paul says the rest of people (nonbelievers) do, has a dark and ominous ring about it (v. 13). The words "no hope" clearly suggest the end, the absence of any future, and a disturbing impotence in the face of it. These words mean despair, discouragement, and at best a fatalistic acceptance. An ancient papyrus from near Paul's time contains the condolences from a parent whose child had died, to another friend whose child, too, had passed away: "I sorrowed and wept over your dear departed one as I wept over Didymas … but really, there is nothing one can do in the face of such things." The sense of defeat and resignation here captures well the non-Christian world's general sense of hopelessness in the face of death. Bluntly and hopelessly, a third-century poet, Theocritus, sums this spirit up well: "Hopes are for the living, the dead are without hope."

Paul, however, does not want these new believers in Christ to continue to wallow unnecessarily in the murky waters of hopeless unbelief. So then, how do those who have hope grieve the loss of believing loved ones? Ignorance of gospel truths, whether from lack of information or forgetfulness, has caused some confusion among these young believers. Paul now focuses their hearts and minds on the great gospel realities that will fill their mourning of loved ones with the kind of hope only faith in Christ gives.

Resurrection of Jesus

It is one thing to claim hope in the face of death—as many do—but it is quite another thing to have solid grounds for such hopeful claims. Many build their hopes on the basis of myths and legendary stories, while others appeal to personal experiences, such as dreams or near-death visions. None of these root their hope in the soil of reality, but rely on the flimsy foundations of the endlessly creative human imagination.

In 1 Thessalonians 4:14, Paul begins by laying the firm foundation of Christian hope in the historical reality of Jesus' death and resurrection—not in some fanciful myth or legend. As the saying goes, "Myths don't make martyrs." There is no near-death experience for someone executed by crucifixion. Roman crucifixion had a 100 percent effectiveness death rate. The truth of Jesus' death is unquestioned. Nor do dazed disciples, dreams, grave robbers, or visions explain away the empty tomb and the appearances of Jesus after his brutal death on the cross. Despite thousands of years of attempts to disprove or reinterpret the biblical witnesses to Jesus' bodily resurrection from the dead, this unique and foundational space-and-time historical truth of Christian faith remains solid and unshaken. It still stands as the starting point for authentic faith in Jesus.

It is what Paul says "we believe," pointing to a personal stand of trusting faith. Rachel was just seven years old when she, helped by her mother one evening, confessed her own faith in Jesus' death and resurrection for her as her Savior and Lord. What a joy to see her faith develop and mature in loving and obedient ways, becoming more and more like Jesus. One of our prized possessions remains Rachel's first Easter card she made for us. In it she wrote: "To Mom and Dad ... you're the best parents anyone could ever want. I hope you have a happy Easter. And I know what the real meaning of Easter is. It's the day Jesus rose from the dead." She had illustrated her card with a childlike drawing of three crosses on a hill, an empty tomb, and a sunrise. Could there ever be a better Easter for parents?

OUR FUTURE STANDS SECURE, FOR IT STANDS IN GOD'S SALVATION HISTORY, IN CHRIST AND THE POWER OF GOD WHO RAISED HIM.

Seven years later, Rachel's last Lord's Day with us here was Easter Sunday, 1999. I remember standing in church and singing together as a family the words of a chorus: "Because He lives, I can face tomorrow."

Many people, struggling with what to say to us, have voiced the sentiment, "I don't know how you can deal with it." A crucial part of the response to that implied question is in the words of that simple song of faith, words that point to a future hope.

It is the song of all believers throughout the ages grieving loved ones who have "fallen asleep in [Jesus]"—a suggestive way of saying they died having trusted in Jesus' death and resurrection work for them. "Sleep" plainly points to anticipation of the time when they will "wake up." The text literally says they die "through" Jesus, a vivid way of explaining a Christian's unity with him. This oneness with Jesus in his death also extends to oneness with him in his resurrection (see Rom. 6:5, 8). Paul views the death of a believer *through* Jesus as but the prelude to being raised again *with* Christ. So, our future stands secure, for it stands in God's salvation history, *in Christ* and the power of God who raised him.

Return of the King

But while a believer's hope is firmly grounded in history, in Jesus' resurrection, that same hope is also anchored to the second coming of Christ when it will be fully realized. After the risen Lord Jesus appeared to literally hundreds of eyewitnesses (see 1 Cor. 15:6), he spoke to his closest followers one last time, assuring them of the presence of his Holy Spirit and commissioning them to be witnesses everywhere of his death and resurrection (see Acts 1:4–11). Then Jesus ascended to heaven. Riveted in place while straining to see him ascending, two angels ("men dressed in white") broke the spell on Jesus' followers with these words: "This same Jesus, who has been taken from you into heaven, will come back in the same way you have seen him go into heaven" (Acts 1:11). Looking back on Jesus' own teaching about the promise of his second coming (1 Thess. 4:15), Paul now shifts attention to the prophetic fulfillment of that promise to descend again one day.

ONE DAY JESUS HIMSELF WILL COME BACK TO OUR SHORES. HE HAS NOT FORGOTTEN US NOR LEFT US, EVEN IN THE MEANWHILE GIVING US HIS SPIRIT AS A COMFORTER.

Paul affirms that "the Lord himself" (v. 16) will descend from heaven. It will be no deputy, but "this same Jesus" himself—no other—

will *personally* come back to fulfill the salvation work he had begun. On March 11, 1942, while leaving Corregidor Island in the Philippines, General MacArthur uttered the famous words: "I shall return." He promised a personal return that implied the deliverance and full freedom of the Philippine people from their oppressors. He was not abandoning them nor forgetting their plight. He would return. MacArthur did return, bringing freedom once again to those shores. One day Jesus himself will come back to our shores. He has not forgotten us or left us, even in the meanwhile giving us his Spirit as a comforter. And he brings full deliverance and freedom—the emphatic and visible return of the King.

In 1 Thessalonians 4:16–17, Paul describes elements of the second coming of the Lord: a loud command, an archangel's voice, a trumpet call, and clouds. Together these words tell us that at his second coming Jesus will return *powerfully* to fulfill his work of redemption for those who love him. At his return, King Jesus issues firm commands, and an archangel announces his victory with a shout. The trumpet call of God summons his people throughout the ages to gather, to come home (see Isa. 27:13; Joel 2:1; Zech. 9:14; Matt. 24:31). The clouds signify the very presence of almighty God, the Ancient of Days, intimately associated with the appearance of the Son of Man, Jesus (see Dan. 7:13). Altogether, these end-times images tell us that Jesus is powerfully able to intervene for his people's full salvation. He has not forgotten. The King will return.

Reunion of the Forever Family

Relating to one another in close family relationships remains one of the purest joys of life. And home is where we experience most intimately that shared life.

Entering our home for the first time following our daughter's death brought an agonizing sense of absence. Seeing and touching her personal effects—a pillow, a pair of shoes, clothes—only intensified the sense of a gaping hole now tangibly felt in our family and home. The feeling of emptiness can almost overwhelm a soul, as if a part of yourself is torn out and you're left gasping for air. I wanted nothing more than to hold her again, to see her glide so effortlessly over the high hurdles again, to hear her joyful laughter again, and to pop the volleyball back and forth again—just to *be with* each other again. No passion grips the soul of one who grieves a loved one more than the desire to be together again.

NO ONE AND NOTHING—NOT EVEN DEATH ITSELF—CAN STAND IN THE WAY OF JESUS TAKING HIS OWN TO BE WITH HIM.

Jesus' second coming comforts and encourages those who grieve especially because it promises a wonderful family reunion. The pain of separation and the loss of relationship are resolved once and for all when Jesus returns. For at the second coming God will resurrect his people throughout the ages who have trusted in him—those who have died first and then those believers still living. No believer, living or dead, will be left out or behind in any way (see 1 Thess. 4:16–17). The whole family of faith will attend!

At Jesus' second coming, all God's people will be "caught up" (v. 17)—a term that refers to a powerful seizing—to meet the Lord in the air. The word *rapture*, drawn from the Latin of this text, is often used to describe this event. Paul does not sink into speculative details about the rapture and Jesus' second coming but accents the sure promise that all believers will be taken by the all-powerful Lord into his own presence. No one and nothing—not even death itself—can stand in the way of Jesus taking his own to be with him.

Furthermore, Paul emphasizes that this great homecoming will be experienced together as the family of God: "We ... will be caught up *together with them*" (v. 17). Paul dramatically concludes with the comforting truth that the pain of separation will then be over and our relationships restored permanently: "*And so we will be with the Lord forever*" (v. 17). The home that once felt empty will be replaced by a new home where we get together again, eternally.

In light of such hope-filled comfort, is it any wonder that Paul concludes by telling them to "encourage each other with these words" (v. 18)?

CHALLENGE: GOING ON LIVING AGAIN (1 THESS. 5:1–11)

Paul, however, wisely takes his encouragement a step further from the comfort of getting together again one day and goes on to the *challenge to go on living again*. And it is a necessary challenge, for there are real temptations to pull away from life.

On one hand, the devastation of grief over the loss of a loved one can numb you to the point of being immobilized. After such loss, going on with the normal affairs of living can hold far less allure than it once did. Getting "back to normal" seems an empty goal, void of interest and energy. We all need appropriate time to heal—a period of real lowness of spirit is to be expected—but lingering long term in such a state, disconnecting from ongoing life and relationships, is not healthy for anyone.

Then, too, how tempting it can be, in light of the future hope of Jesus' second coming and the restoration of relationships, to sit back and wait for the arrival of that great day of the Lord when all wrongs will be righted. Understandably, the day of the Lord (1 Thess. 5:2)—best seen as a period of God's righteous judgment begun at the second coming of

Christ—captivates the hearts and minds of God's people. However, an unhealthy fixation on it and its timing can lead to a dangerously passive disconnection from the life God has given us in the here and now. In 1 Thessalonians 5:1–11, Paul addresses this real-life concern.

Aware

First of all in 1 Thessalonians 5:1–5, Paul appeals to the fact that they are not in the dark about the matter of Jesus' second coming. Though God has not revealed the exact timing of Jesus' return, Paul reminds the Thessalonian believers of what they do know. They are aware that the day of the Lord will indeed come. Drawing on Jesus' own teaching using the imagery of the thief in the night (see Matt. 24:36–44), Paul underlines the fact that while Jesus' return may catch unbelievers unsuspecting, God's people fully expect his coming again. Given such certain knowledge, and given also the reality that no person knows the day or the hour of the Lord's return, how then should we live in the meanwhile? The very fact that God has seen fit to continue giving us life makes this question crucial, for it tells us there is divinely ordained purpose for our lives.

Armed and Ready

Echoing Jesus' own teaching on his second coming, Paul calls Christians to be vigilant. In 1 Thessalonians 5:6–8, he draws a strong pairs contrast between unbelievers who are sleepy or drunk and believers who are alert or self-controlled (sober). The point of this double contrast is that while non-Christians act inappropriately and lack responsible control, believers must live responsibly and appropriately in God's sight—especially in view of Jesus' sure return.

Paul immediately goes on to shed light on *how* believers should go on living in a way that is proper and pleasing to God (v. 8). The apostle pic-turesquely says such living must put on the essential Christian virtues of faith, hope, and love like pieces of armor for a soldier going into battle.

Protecting the vital parts of the torso, faith and love serve as a sort of heavy metal breastplate that will deflect the piercing blows aimed at the heart. Guarding the head, salvation's hope acts like a helmet sheltering our minds from the assaults of doubt, fear, and guilt. Clearly the challenge to "watch" (v. 6 KJV), alert and self-controlled, has nothing to do with passively observing, but has everything to do with purposefully and actively engaging life in a way that pleases God. So, God's Word calls us to be spiritually armed and ready for battles yet to be fought on the fields of life.

> GOD LEADS PEOPLE
> IN DIFFERENT WAYS
> TO EMBRACE LIFE
> ANEW, BUT THOSE
> WAYS INVARIABLY
> WILL INVOLVE THE
> DEMONSTRATION OF
> GENUINE FAITH,
> LOVE, AND HOPE.

Following the loss of our daughter, we experienced the emotions of disconnection and the resulting temptation to withdraw from life and relationships. But this biblical teaching about Jesus' second coming not only comforted us but also challenged us to live again in the very ways of faith, love, and hope that would honor Rachel's memory and the Lord who gave her to us for a time. What, practically, would this mean for us? How could we embrace life again, giving faith, hope, and love tangibly real expression in our home? Since Rachel embodied for our family a relationship filled with these joyous spiritual fruits, a relationship that mirrored the heart of God himself, why not bring that kind of family relationship experience to someone who does not have it?

This passion led us ultimately on a journey of love to adopt two baby girls from China, a visible, ongoing expression of us embracing life again—with faith, love, and hope. God leads people in different ways to embrace life anew, but those ways invariably will involve the demonstration of genuine faith, love, and hope.

THE ENCOURAGEMENT OF JESUS' SECOND COMING BRINGS BOTH THE COMFORT OF RESTORED RELATIONSHIPS AS WELL AS THE CHALLENGE TO GO ON LIVING AGAIN FOR HIM.

Assured

Paul then explains *why* believers can live in this way (5:9–10). God himself has planned—"appoint[ed]"—that his people know salvation from sin through Jesus' death for them. However, the destiny of God's children is not only to die to sin and death through faith in Jesus' death for them, but also to "live together with" Christ (v. 10, an echo of 4:17). And no matter what, whether we die first or remain alive until Jesus' return, that destiny stands eternally secure in the person of Jesus. Our relationship with him can no more be shaken than God's own will for our salvation in the Lord Jesus Christ can be broken. With this powerful assurance, Paul strengthens any wavering resolve for the battles of life that yet lie before us.

Again, as before in 4:18, it is no surprise that Paul concludes this message by urging them to "encourage one another" (5:11). The encouragement of Jesus' second coming brings both the comfort of restored relationships as well as the challenge to go on living again for him.

Where Is the Hope?

From the earliest days of the ancient church, Christians have believed in, and longed passionately for, Jesus' return as our "blessed hope" (Titus 2:13)—hope realized fully in the future by the renewal of relationship with Jesus and beloved fellow believers; hope realized now by active, purposeful lives given over to tangible expressions of faith, love, and hope.

In Revelation 22:20, the risen Lord gives an affirmation that his people's prayers will be answered with the promise, "Yes, I am coming soon." This promise at once elicits the prayerful cry of believers yearning for his coming: "Amen. Come, Lord Jesus." His promise is the sum of all promises, an assurance of Christ's abiding presence for us and with us. That prayer is the sum of all living hope, the cry for the coming of the kingdom of God—the return of the King.

"HERE IS MY HEART, LORD ..."

Sometimes worry and anxiety about the future cloud my grieving when I think about the death of my loved one, Lord, but my grieving is colored by hope because ...

Although my spirit can be understandably low because of my loss, Jesus, the most encouraging thing to me as I contemplate your return is that ...

Lord, when I think of your loud command, the archangel's voice, the trumpet of God blasting, and your coming on clouds, I know that this time your coming ...

Lord Jesus, my grief is tinged with joy knowing that not one of your people, alive or dead, will be left behind, because this means that ...

However much I might feel like disconnecting from people and life itself, knowing that you are coming back—and that I am still here—I ...

When the topic of your return comes up, Lord, give me wisdom and boldness to share with others that ...

Chapter 10

IN THE TWINKLING
OF AN EYE

——❦ 1 CORINTHIANS 15 ❦——

*How do our loved ones who have died as believers live
on? Just in memories? Just in the various tokens of their
lives we still have to treasure—a bracelet they wore, a
picture drawn and colored for Father's Day, a favorite
toy, or a special dress? However much we treasure those
painfully sweet tokens and memories, hope does not rest
in these. No, Paul teaches us we will be changed one
day to "bear the likeness of the man from heaven," Jesus
(1 Cor. 15:49). But how can this be?*

Going to the cemetery to care for and place flowers on Rachel's grave
always affects us deeply. Taking our two little preschool daughters
along presents additional challenges to an already tough task. Though
well behaved and even helpful (usually), the observant and precocious
older preschooler often peppers us with awkward, if insightful, questions.
On one occasion, as we neared the graveyard, the four-year-old asked,
"Daddy, where is Rachel now?" I kept my answer brief and to the point.
"If she's in heaven," she followed up looking puzzled, "then why do we

go to the cemetery all the time?" Soberly I explained about graveyards, gravestones, and burying the bodies of people who die, though I quickly added that people like Rachel who loved and trusted Jesus in this life go on living with him right away in heaven. She took this in but continued to press for more. "So," she asked with furrowed forehead, forming her next question, "how does she get around in heaven?" And so such conversations go as she works hard to wrap her acute and agile young mind around age-old enigmas, concerns, eternal truths, and, of course, more questions.

JESUS' RESURRECTION STANDS AS THE KEYSTONE OF OUR FAITH AND HOPE, PULLING TOGETHER EVERYTHING WE KNOW OF HIM FROM START TO FINISH.

Questions among the young believers in Corinth concerning resurrection, death, the body, and the afterlife led to confused conclusions among some there. In 1 Corinthians 15, Paul orients his response to them around two questions seen in that passage (vv. 12, 35) that reveal their confusion. On one hand, they likely saw the resurrection for believers as a past *spiritual* experience (v. 12), denying any future resurrection to come at all—a belief, as seen in 2 Timothy 2:18, that would continue to plague Paul's churches with destructive consequences for faith. On a closely related line, they also could not conceive of any continued *bodily* existence after death (v. 35). Here then Paul, in his longest sustained teaching on resurrection (1 Cor. 15), corrects such confused and dangerous thinking with clear gospel truths that will strengthen, not destroy, their faith and hope.

Today confusion about resurrection and afterlife runs rampant, with people holding a host of disconnected ideas and wild speculations. People are fascinated by and advocate all sorts of possibilities, from various rein-carnation theories, to vague near-death "light" experiences, to circle-of-life organic recycling hypotheses, to science-fictional explana-tions, and of course to the outright denials given by some scientific camps committed to antisupernaturalism. Even more confusingly, in our plural-istic age, every option is open and often held (incoherently) at the same time. Worse, even some "Christian" teachers contribute to the confusion by denying Jesus' real bodily resurrection, seeing it as a nonhistorical lit-erary myth that merely reveals spiritual truth. How similar this all looks to the confusion of the Corinthians two thousand years ago.

Why not look carefully at what the Bible says? In short, Paul teaches us that one day believers in Jesus will also be raised with resurrection bodies just like his. More fully, in this passage Paul shows us that as believers who know the *certainty* of Jesus' resurrection, we can have hope because we are *connected* to him in his resurrection and will be *changed* to be like the risen Lord Jesus when he comes again. These three great affirmations of hope give us strength, hold us firm in faith, and energize our effective living for the Lord now (v. 58).

I Am Certain ... of Jesus' Bodily Resurrection (1 Cor. 15:1–11)

Concerned that the Corinthian believers were veering off course in their faith, Paul begins by reminding them of the core of Christian faith and the ground zero of gospel hope—Jesus' resurrection from the dead (vv. 1–2). Apart from it, Paul contends, their faith would be in vain; the gospel hope itself would collapse into an empty husk. So Paul begins by reminding them of the *certainty of Jesus' real bodily resurrection*, confirm-ing it by a chain of eyewitnesses to the risen Lord, beginning with Peter and ending with Paul himself (vv. 5–8). Such eyewitness testimonies debunk any notion of a disembodied resurrected Jesus. The Gospels all show this, for the tomb was empty, and, later, Thomas was invited by Jesus to touch his hands. Jesus even ate food with them. His was a real and bodily resurrection. (Notably, Paul also mentions that some believers have already died, but by saying that they have "fallen asleep" [v. 6], he anticipates the key truth of 1 Corinthians 15 that they, too, will awaken and arise in resurrection themselves!)

CHRIST'S RESURRECTION CANNOT BE DISCONNECTED IN ANY WAY FROM A BELIEVER'S OWN FUTURE BODILY RESURRECTION.

Interestingly, Paul was the last to see the risen Jesus. He compares himself to a stillborn child (premature and dead) brought from death to life only by a miracle (v. 8). Paul saw himself also as *least* of the eyewitnesses, for when he saw Jesus—unlike all the other witnesses—he was yet in unbelief and was a persecutor of Christians. So as one who was both dead and despicable when he saw Jesus, Paul humbly presents himself as an example of a walking gospel miracle, a witness to the resurrection power and life-changing grace of God (vv. 9–10). He owes everything to Christ. His effective gospel work was pure grace. He is like a child who goes out and buys his dad a great gift for Father's Day—with the money his dad gave him. It is all grace, and Paul knew it.

Easter of 1999 was the last Sunday with my daughter in church, the great day on which believers specially celebrate Jesus' resurrection from the dead—and the defeat of death and the birth of hope. As our family sat together, we worshipped with scriptural teachings that told again the story of Jesus rising from the grave. We affirmed our faith in his resurrection through word and song: "I serve a risen Savior; he's in the world today. I *know* that he is living, whatever men may say." In various ways, together we confessed anew out loud and within ourselves, "*I am certain that Jesus rose from the dead.*" As believers, we gather to worship on Sunday because of the resurrection, and as I think back on my last Sunday with Rachel, sharing our faith in the risen Lord Jesus on Easter Sunday, Jesus' resurrection always specially colors my sorrow with heavenly hues of hope. No wonder Charles Wesley emphatically punctuated every line of his great Easter hymn, "Christ the Lord Is Risen Today," with the repeated exclamation mark of triumph and hope: "Alleluia!" Jesus' resurrection stands as the keystone of our faith and hope, pulling together everything we know of him from start to finish. Without it, Christian faith falls apart. Even Christmas and Calvary become venues of hope solely because of Jesus' victory once for all over sin and death.

I Am Connected ... to Jesus in His Resurrection (1 Cor. 15:12–34)

Having reminded them of the certainty of Jesus' bodily resurrection—a faith stand the believers in Corinth did affirm—Paul now builds on this foundational truth to address two problems (15:12 and 15:35) they had in applying this truth to themselves. On one hand, they had neatly isolated Jesus' bodily resurrection from their own, regarding resurrection for believers as solely a spiritual experience already over and done with in the present. Denying any future resurrection for believers, some said, "There is no resurrection of the dead" (v. 12). Paul views with deep concern any such disconnection between the Lord Jesus and those who belong to him. He sees it as deadly for faith and hope. Therefore, he takes great pains (vv. 12–34) to explore the central truth of authentic Christian faith: "*I am connected to Jesus.*" This connection extends ultimately to a believer's solidarity with him in bodily resurrection from the dead.

Full Unity, Not Futility (vv. 13–20)

Paul begins with a series of relentlessly logical "if-then" statements that point to the inescapable truth that a believer is fully united with Jesus in his resurrection from the dead (15:13–19). Christ's resurrection cannot be disconnected in any way from a believer's own future bodily resurrection. They are intimately connected. To make sure no one misses his point, Paul patiently circles back and repeats his thoughts (vv. 15–19 parallel 13–15), putting emphasis again and again on the one central truth upon which faith and hope ultimately depend for believers. Jesus' resurrection and ours stand or fall together, inextricably connected, and since Jesus' resurrection stands, so, too, does ours! To deny our bodily resurrection can only result in spiritual emptiness and pitiful hopelessness. But Paul abruptly pulls away from that dead end for hope and faith, again affirming the ground of his hope-filled faith: "But Christ has indeed been raised from the dead" (v. 20).

Firstfruits and Harvest Hope (vv. 20–23)

Paul then illustrates that critical connection of the believer to Jesus and develops it even further. He starts with a well-known religious ritual practiced in both the Jewish and Greco-Roman worlds—offering up the "firstfruits" of a harvest. The Old Testament (Lev. 23:10–11) prescribed that the harvest's first sheaf of grain be brought to the temple as an offering to the Lord. Paul calls Jesus the "firstfruits of those who have fallen asleep" (1 Cor. 15:20). Paul uses this metaphor for Jesus' resurrection because it implies *more to come* (quantity), the first sheaf carrying with it the sure promise of the far larger part yet to be harvested. Furthermore, it indicates that the harvest will yield *more of the same kind* (quality) of fruit or grain. Paul focuses on the link between the "firstfruits" and the rest of the harvest to come—an inseparable connection that guarantees more to come and more of the same kind of thing. Paul draws out this connection between Jesus and his people, here in relation to resurrection. Jesus' resurrection was first (and greatest), a pledge of the larger resurrection harvest yet to come in its own turn (v. 23). Then, too, that harvest would yield more fruit of the same kind, more "fruit" like that which Jesus' resurrection represented—more "resurrection bodies" like Jesus' own for those who "belong to him" (v. 23). Seen, then, as "firstfruits," Jesus' resurrection yields for believers a "harvest hope."

First and Last Adam (vv. 21–22)

OUR FUTURE BODILY
RESURRECTION
MUST IMPACT THE
WAY WE CONDUCT
OURSELVES IN THIS
PRESENT WORLD.

Still trying to explain the idea of our connection to Jesus, Paul points to the first man, Adam (15:21–22; see also Rom. 5:12–20). He links every human in history back to Adam, naturally and by choice (choosing to sin by loving self rather than God). That

connection results, Paul says concisely, in death for everyone: "*In Adam* all die." On the other hand, believers have a new and higher connection. By faith they now are linked to the "last Adam" (1 Cor. 15:45), Jesus Christ, now *super*naturally and by choice (choosing to love and trust the Lord above all). This connection to Christ results, Paul says, in resurrection life and the defeat of death for everyone who dies as a believer: "*In Christ* all will be made alive." In both cases there is a linkage and a heritage, but for a Christian the connection to Jesus, the "last Adam," brings resurrected life and supersedes the connection to the "first Adam," which only brings death.

Final Curtain of Salvation Drawn (vv. 23–28)

Ultimately, Paul rests his hope in God the Father, who set into motion a whole chain of events to bring people back into relationship with himself. This redemptive drama has played out all through human history, from Adam to Abraham, from the Jewish people, their prophets, priests, and kings to the Messiah, Jesus—the incarnation of God himself. But the final act of salvation's drama begins with Jesus' resurrection and climaxes when all believers receive their resurrection bodies at Jesus' second coming. Jesus will vanquish every hostile force in the universe, and "then *the end* will come." Completing salvation's goal (end) Jesus delivers the final blow to the "last enemy," death, at his second coming, when all his people are raptured and rise up in resurrected bodies to meet him—the connection to Christ now complete, the relationship fully restored.

THOUGH RADICALLY CHANGED, WE WILL STILL BE ABLE TO RECOGNIZE ONE ANOTHER IN HEAVEN. SO, WITH GREAT HOPE, WE MAY JOYFULLY ANTICIPATE BEING TOGETHER AGAIN *PERSONALLY* WITH LOVED ONES IN CHRIST WHO HAVE DIED.

Future Matters Now (vv. 29–34)

Paul finally concludes with some examples that show how such a connection with Christ in his bodily resurrection in the future affects the way we live now. Whether referring to the bizarre practice—which he does not endorse—of baptizing people on behalf of believers who died before they could be baptized (15:29) or referring to his own willingness to die for the gospel (vv. 30–32), Paul knows that our future bodily resurrection must impact the way we conduct ourselves in this present world. The Epicurean "live it up" philosophy is not an option for people of the resurrection (v. 32). Nor should believers keep company with false teachers who mislead people about the resurrection, for eventually it will corrupt their lives and compromise the quality of their relationship to Christ (v. 33). Paul ends this part by calling them to "sober up" (v. 34 NJB) and think straight—and therefore walk straight as well.

I WILL BE CHANGED ... TO BE LIKE THE RISEN LORD JESUS (1 COR. 15:35–58)

At the beginning of the last part of 1 Corinthians 15, Paul anticipates a question (v. 35) concerning the *nature* of the resurrection body: "How are the dead raised? With what kind of body will they come?" Everyone knew that human flesh decomposed, so how could life after death be "bodily"? Whether in puzzlement or mockery here, the question was raised—and continues to arise in people's minds today. While rejecting the temptation to squeeze out of the text what is not there, Paul's clear teaching about the resurrection body resonates sonorous notes of hope.

Designed for Eternity (vv. 36–49)

Paul sternly begins by calling this hypothetical question downright "foolish" (15:36). But it is not simply a matter of ignorance, for Paul likely is thinking of the "fool" of Psalm 14:1: "The fool says in his heart, 'There is no God.'" The question itself shows they have not taken the God of creation into account. Paul now corrects this glaring omission, teaching them about the "spiritual body" (1 Cor. 15:44) that God himself will resurrect.

Analogies from Creation (vv. 36–42)

Paul begins by using several analogies from creation to illustrate insights into the nature of the mysterious resurrection body. In turn he looks at agriculture, animals, and astronomy.

Paul first points them to the farmer in his field who sows seeds in the ground (15:36–38). Everyone knew that on the very spot the farmer sowed a dried-up little seed, a very different-looking, lush plant would rise upward. The dry old seed buried in the ground has an undeniable continuity with the great plant that grows from it, though difference (discontinuity) captures our attention most. The ancient botanist Paul wants to make one simple point: *Change* happens! A small seed blooms in abundant harvest. Leaving aside the details of "how," Paul focuses on God as the transformer behind this major change. God takes what looks to have little hope for a glorious body (the "seed" of mortal flesh) and with creative power raises up a great plant (the "harvest" of a changed resurrection body). God has both the *will* and the *power* to do this.

On a final note of interest, many of us wonder whether we will be recognizable in our resurrected form. Will I be identifiably me? That each seed has it "own" (v. 38) body that fits it perfectly points to a positive answer. Even as a little boy growing up on a farm in South Dakota, I knew that when you planted a bare corn seed a cornstalk would grow—not oats or wheat, but corn. I could see they were the same, however different the later tall stalk looked from the seed sown before. The corn seed had its "own" body. Yes, though radically changed, we will still be able to recognize one another in heaven. So, with great hope, we may joyfully anticipate being together again *personally* with loved ones in Christ who have died.

Paul next looks at animals ("earthly bodies" of "flesh") and astronomy ("heavenly bodies" of "splendor") to help them better understand the resurrection body (vv. 39–41). By listing a variety of animals and celestial spheres, Paul simply points to the fact that God can and does make different kinds of bodies—one more kind of body (resurrected) would prove no problem for the God who hung the stars in space! Paul also contrasts the earthly/fleshly bodies (v. 39) with the heavenly/splendor bodies (v. 41), making the point that resurrection (heavenly) bodies are vastly different from our earthly bodies. God will not merely recycle old flesh cells and resuscitate me but will miraculously transform me into a radically different and radiant "body" fit for heaven—*designed for eternity.*

Attributes of the "Spiritual" (Resurrection) Body (vv. 42–44)

The radical transformation of our bodies has become big business in America with plastic surgeons raking in piles of money from people unhappy with one part or many parts of their anatomy. So-called reality TV shows pander to this powerful desire to change our bodies, offering up dazzling menus of tummy tucks, nose jobs, face-lifts, bottom-lifts ... sucking some out here, putting some in there, hair plucking here, and hair plugging there. But how paltry this looks when compared to the radical change, the whole "body-lift," to come for believers in Christ.

Using four contrasting pairs (15:42–44), Paul emphasizes the radical difference between our attributes as humankind and our attributes as heaven-kind. In our Adamic humanity ("the body that is sown") we are all perishable, dishonored, weak, and natural. In our heavenly resurrection body, we are raised imperishable, glorious, powerful, and supernatural ("spiritual"). No wonder Paul, in a later letter (2 Cor. 5), compares our earthly body to a mere tent to be folded up, while our heavenly body is like an "eternal house in heaven." Who among us does not look forward to a body free from decay, disabilities, disease, and death? As believers we cry out with sure hope and joyous anticipation, "Vive la difference!" The book of Revelation climaxes with the heart of this great hope: "He will wipe every tear from their eyes. There will be no more death or mourning or crying or pain, for the old order of things has passed away" (21:4).

Appropriate Body for a Heavenly Habitat (vv. 44–49)

With our connection to Adam on his mind, Paul now (15:45) quotes Genesis 2:7. This key Old Testament text recounts Adam's creation from the dust of the earth when God breathed life into his "natural body"—a body that soon fell into sin, bringing death and separation from God. This terrible Adamic heritage has since been passed down to every human being. It is where we all "live," bearing the broken likeness of Adam, our forefather, in a "natural body." Paul addresses their bewilderment over how an earthly body formed from dirt and fallen in sin could ever be fit for a heavenly environment. But Paul points them back again to their new faith connection to Jesus Christ, the last and perfect Adam (man) who is a "life-giving spirit"—resurrection life! He comes "from heaven," meaning his origin and character are heavenly and divine. As "last Adam," Jesus also passes a heritage on to those who belong to him, for they shall be like "the man from heaven," Jesus (15:48–49). In finally and fully bearing his likeness, when Jesus returns, they, too, will receive transformed resurrected bodies—real, substantial "spiritual bodies," perfectly appropriate for a heavenly habitat, *designed for eternity* there with the Lord.

Dressed for Heaven (vv. 50–58)

Paul now summarizes everything he has been teaching the Corinthians. Paul grants that they were right in saying frail, corrupt bodies could not possibly inherit the imperishable heavenly kingdom of God (15:50). But they had jumped to the wrong conclusion from this by denying any future bodily life after death (resurrection) for the believer. Throughout 1 Corinthians 15, Paul carefully corrects this error, teaching them the divinely revealed "mystery" that God will radically transform their bodies to resurrected "spiritual bodies," appropriately dressed for heaven.

What Must Happen (vv. 50–53)

Growing up with pigs, cattle, and other animals, I had ample opportunity to get seriously dirty. Mom worked diligently at cleaning me up, but it was an uphill battle. On Saturday nights, however, I got the full treatment because Sunday was coming. And Sunday morning, my regular old work and play clothes—inappropriate for the Lord's house—had to go. "Sunday clothes" and a cleaned-up version of me were a *necessity* for going to church on Sunday.

Paul knew frail and fallen human bodies could not survive in the heavenly presence of God, as if merely moving to a better neighborhood. But neither would we become wispy vapors wafting in the skies. Though hidden from humanity's understanding before, Paul has been teaching them throughout 1 Corinthians 15 the mystery now revealed by God. God himself will *change* every believer in Jesus—alive at the time or dead—into resurrected "spiritual bodies" like Christ's, perfectly fitted to heaven. Transformation must take place. It will not be a process but will happen instantaneously—"in a flash, in the twinkling of an eye"

THE RESURRECTION DRAINS THE DEADLY, POISONOUS "STING" OF DEATH AND ITS CLOSE ALLY, SIN, OF THEIR POWER OVER US. WE SHALL BE FINALLY AND COMPLETELY FREE AT LAST.

(v. 52)—when the last trumpet blows and Jesus triumphantly returns. Paul illustrates this miraculous change with a clothing metaphor, getting *dressed for heaven.* God, the ultimate quick-change artist, will "put on" the new imperishable and immortal body over our old mortal body, another interesting way of showing how we will continue on as the same person, though radically changed.

What Will Happen (vv. 54–58)

Paul now finishes his lengthy resurrection teaching by saying that when it happens, humanity's ancient foe—death itself—will have been finally vanquished. In 15:54 Paul quotes Isaiah to give the prophetic picture of death being "swallowed up"—utterly defeated—in the victory of the resurrection. In verse 55 Paul breaks out in rhapsody as he then freely quotes Hosea 13:14, mocking death's powerlessness in the face of God's grace through Jesus' work on the cross and in the resurrection. The resurrection drains the deadly, poisonous "sting" of death and its close ally, sin, of their power over us. We shall be finally and completely free at last, thanks to God's victory for us in Jesus. For now, we are newly empowered to remain firm in our faith, fully devoted to living now for Christ in light of the resurrection and eternity.

OUR FUNERALS SHOULD LOOK FORWARD TO THE "HOMEGOING" OF OUR BELIEVING LOVED ONES, COLORING OUR SORROWS WITH JOY AND HOPE.

Where Is the Hope?

In this passage Paul has provided us with three great affirmations of hope that can sustain us no matter what may come. Hope for the believer in Jesus was born on Easter morning when the stone was rolled away and Jesus rose from the dead. *I am certain* of this ground of grace and hope. I have hope now because *I am connected* to Jesus, since I died in him to my sin and will rise in him in resurrected life as well. Finally, I look forward with joyous hope to his second coming when at last *I will be changed* to be like Christ in his resurrection body, living forever in the very presence of God. There is no greater hope than this perfect consummation of our relationship with the Lord. As believers, therefore, we may put fear aside. Though we yet grieve the deaths of loved ones in Christ and our own future well-being may hold uncertainties, still our grieving and concerns are not like those of people "who have no hope" (1 Thess. 4:13). Our funerals should look forward to the "homegoing" of our believing loved ones, coloring our sorrows with joy and hope. And the promise of our future resurrection creates a hope-filled, eager expectation for that day when Jesus returns and when our relationship with him and all other believers who have gone on before us will reach truly heavenly proportions. "Thanks be to God! He gives us the victory through our Lord Jesus Christ" (1 Cor. 15:57).

"HERE IS MY HEART, LORD ..."

Lord, when I think of my loved ones who have died, I remember your own resurrection from the dead on Easter, and it reminds me that ...

Jesus, seeing the way Paul includes himself as "last" and "least" of the eyewitnesses of your resurrection encourages me because ...

To know that you, Jesus, are the "firstfruits" of the resurrection brings real hope to my soul because it means ...

Lord, I still feel the troubling reality of my connection to the "first man Adam," especially when I ...

Dear God, I confess that sometimes I've acted like the "fool" of Psalm 14:1 who forgets to take into account your power, love, and wisdom—especially during dark times of loss, such as when I ...

The next time, Lord, that I plant a "seed," I will meditate on this passage about the resurrection again and remember with hope that ...

Oh Lord God, I so long for the day when I, too, will be changed to receive my resurrection body at Jesus' second coming, especially because this means that ...

Dear Jesus, I know that many people fear death, so lead me to someone who is struggling in this way and help me to share with him or her from this passage that ...

Chapter 11

HOPE: A MATTER OF LIFE OR DEATH

❦ PHILIPPIANS 1:12–26 ❧

*Writing from prison, Paul ponders two possible out-
comes for himself—life or death. Hope colors how Paul
views these alternatives, a viewpoint captured in his
poignantly concise confession: "For to me, to live is
Christ and to die is gain" (Phil. 1:21). In a passage
tinged with surprising joy and confidence, the apostle
invites us all to peer into this window of his soul ...
and to share with him in that same hope.*

He served bravely as an officer in the Soviet Union's army, helping
to turn back the furious Nazi invasion of mother Russia and then
pushing Hitler's forces back to Germany. Yet upon his return home, the
paranoid Stalinist rulers viewed this wartime hero with suspicion. They
promptly arrested him and shipped him off into the notoriously brutal
Russian prison system of work camps scattered throughout Siberia—the
Gulag Archipelago. Years later, after surviving this dehumanizing experience, Alexander Solzhenitsyn took a new weapon, a pen, and wrote a
short novel graphically depicting real life in a Stalinist work camp.

Solzhenitsyn, now a Christian, gives occasional intriguing glimpses in his book of "Baptists" (a Russian term then for any evangelical believer) in the work camp who were being persecuted for their religious beliefs. One such passage in particular has always captured my imagination.

> Far in the distance, on the other side of the site, the sun, red and enormous, was rising in haze, its beams cutting obliquely through the gates, the whole building site, and the fence. Alyosha, who was standing next to Shukhov, gazed at the sun and looked happy, a smile on his lips. What had he to be happy about? His cheeks were sunken, he lived strictly on his rations, he earned nothing. He spent all his Sundays muttering with the other Baptists. They shed the hardships of camp life like water off a duck's back.[1]

Trusting Christ alone and treasuring out loud the truths found on the scraps of Bible pages they had, these imprisoned "muttering Baptists," like Alyosha, had their hearts and bodies broken through terrible suffering and loss, *yet they never lost hope nor even joy.* They had a kindred spirit in another Christian prisoner centuries earlier—the apostle Paul.

Unjustly imprisoned, his trial stalled two years by a corrupt official waiting for a bribe, the energetic apostle Paul could have felt like giving up. Now, having been transferred from Palestine to house arrest in Rome and awaiting an imminent trial before a court of Caesar, Paul also could well have experienced high anxiety and fear as he contemplated the court's upcoming decision on his fate. Yet Paul, allowed pen and papyrus to write to friends, composes a letter to the Philippians that carries no note of bitterness or fear, of disillusionment or anxiety, but veritably breathes a spirit of joy, faith, life-embracing vibrancy, and hope-filled expectancy. How could this be?

In Paul's letter to the Philippians, he wanted his Christian friends there to know more than just news of "what has happened to me" (1:12) and especially to understand *how he views* what has happened to him— the *viewpoint of hope in Christ* that gives him such an indomitable spirit in the face of suffering, loss, and a dangerous trial before Nero's court. Paul wants his readers—the Philippians then and us now—to share his same life-changing framework of hope in the face of suffering and loss. In Philippians 1:12–26, Paul sets himself out as an example. He demonstrates for us that, despite heartbreaking hardships and losses, we can experience hope and joy by (1) learning to turn our bonds into bridges and (2) letting Christ be magnified in us, whether in life or in death. From such a vantage point of Christ-centered faith and hope, Paul exudes confidence, courage, and anticipation of future progress and joy—no matter what might come.

WILL WE TRUST GOD TO HELP US TURN OUR BONDS INTO BRIDGES TO NEW REDEEMING RELATIONSHIPS OF LOVE?

LEARNING TO TURN MY BONDS INTO BRIDGES (PHIL. 1:12–18)

Move Forward ... Despite Being Held Back (vv. 12–14)

Paul reveals a key to his viewpoint of hope by putting the key word *progress* at the beginning of this longer section and again near the end (*advance* [v. 12] and *progress* [v. 25] are the same word in the Greek). This bookend effect stresses the fact that Paul looked at these hard experiences as a time of "progress," a time of moving forward despite being held back by chains.

Chain of Events

It hardly looked like progress at first glance. Paul's two-year imprisonment in Palestine ended abruptly when a change in Roman governors there brought new danger. A political favor would have soon exposed Paul (intentionally) to assassination by his avowed enemies in Jewish leadership, so the Roman citizen Paul appealed to Caesar's court, forcing the Roman governor to comply at once (see Acts 25). Paul was sent to Rome under guard, and, though shipwrecked on Malta, he finally arrived. There in Rome, awaiting trial under house arrest two more years (!), he received guests and corresponded by letters with supporters such as the Philippians (see Acts 28).

Paul wanted them (and us) to know that what could easily have been seen as a dead end became instead a divine appointment for progress. His adversity opened new avenues into the lives of untouched people—especially palace military officials and their extended contacts. Seizing the opportunity, Paul ensured they all knew why he was imprisoned: "I am in chains for Christ" (Phil. 1:13). Rather than hold him back, Paul learned how God would help him turn his bonds into bridges for advancing the good news of Jesus in ways and places he had never imagined. What is more, other believers in Rome saw Paul's example, and they, too, gained courage to stand boldly for Christ in the middle of hard circumstances and a hostile culture (v. 14).

Chain Reaction

We each have our chains that bind us up in one way or another. The bonds are varied: job issues, poverty, harmful addictions, personal-history challenges, health problems, family dysfunction, relationship difficulties, and countless other troubles. We all wrestle with prisons, places in life where we feel bound up, caught, and held. But will we trust God to help us turn those bonds into bridges to new redeeming relationships of love, as Paul did? The Watergate-era example of Chuck Colson rings especially true here. His conversion to faith in Christ and subsequent prison experience became for him a launching pad into a passionate pursuit of sharing the gospel hope with fellow prison inmates. Apparent hindrance opened hopeful horizons for thousands. Other stories, such as the well-known story of Joni Eareckson Tada's paralyzing diving accident, illustrate time and again that bonds can become bridges to new places, opportunities, and people who would never be reached otherwise.

My own "prison" story revolves around the sudden loss of Rachel. In the time following her death, the sense of loss was so pervasive that I felt as if my own life were now at a dead end. My future hopes seemed abruptly extinguished, and it seemed the chains of grief would bind me and choke my life forever.

> I FOUND MY BONDS OF SORROW AND GRIEF THEN TRANSFORMED INTO BRIDGES OF HOPE.

Seemingly held fast by my "bonds," desperate and knowing nowhere else to turn, I returned to God and to his Word, where I heard anew his Spirit's voice speaking from the Scriptures. Saint Augustine said, "God gives where he finds open hands." With my hands and heart wide open, God graciously brought me to passages that touched me in just the right way—sometimes with healing tones and tears, other times with an uplifting anticipation of heaven and the future. But always at every turn, I found faith renewed and hope reawakened.

I found my bonds of sorrow and grief then transformed into bridges of hope. God began to bring people to me over the following years whose struggles with grief and loss of various kinds were like chains in their lives. Whether through letters or direct personal interaction, God allowed me to help them walk through their valleys with a renewed sense of courage and hope. On one occasion, not many months after Rachel's death, I was invited to speak to a youth gathering of several hundred high school students. I was still emotionally shaky, but God strengthened me to tell them how God was healing my heart and to share the way God's Word was restoring my hope. Now, years later, people continue to come and tell me they still remember the impact it made on their whole lives. Many of the Scriptures and thoughts I shared that night became the basis for this book. I pray that through avenues such as these I will continue to learn to let God turn my bonds into biblical bridges of hope, faith, and love in others' lives.

Make the Main Thing … the Main Thing (vv. 15–18)

However uplifting Paul's viewpoint of hope was in Philippians 1:12–14, his following comments (vv. 15–18) feel awkward to us. Evidently some truly Christian people in Rome (a minority who were at odds with Paul for some unstated reason) spoke and acted in ways that were meant to hurt Paul and stir up trouble for him. Though Paul gives no details, terms like "envy," "rivalry," and "selfish ambition" paint a sorry picture of their mean spirits. Worse yet, they did this while Paul was actually still facing hard time in prison—there in defense of the gospel.

How Paul responds to such hurtful fellow believers carries an important lesson. While not ignoring it or condoning it, in verse 18 Paul simply says, "What does it matter?" Despite their lousy motives, evidently their basic message of the gospel itself was accurate about Jesus, and that, Paul concludes, is the important thing. Not only does Paul choose to set aside (for now) their bad behavior and his own personal hurt, but he chooses to focus on and even take joy in the most important thing of all—that "Christ is preached." Paul will let God sort these sorry saints out in his own time. For now, Paul chooses to make the main thing—his hope in Jesus—the main thing.

Why would Paul have shared this? No doubt to prepare the Philippians (and us) for similar attacks. Almost everyone I've talked to concerning loss speaks sadly about others saying and doing things that actually hurt them. Rather than stew over it and become angry, embittered, and disillusioned—a natural reaction—I've learned the wisdom of saying with Paul, "What does it matter?" I find freedom by letting God know my hurt and leaving matters of chastising and teaching others up to him in his own time. Focusing then on my hope in Christ frees me up to be joyful again and continue learning to let God turn my bonds into bridges of hope for those who will hear.

LET CHRIST BE MAGNIFIED IN ME ... WHETHER IN DEATH OR IN LIFE (PHIL. 1:18–26)

Paul now looks beyond his past and present life experiences to ponder his *future*. As before, just *how he views* his life experiences is key to Paul's thoughts and offers us a window into his soul. As he found progress and joy in his past and present tough times (vv. 12–18), Paul looks forward to *progress and joy* in the future also (vv. 18, 25), however his trial turns out. Specifically, Paul confidently anticipates his "deliverance" (v. 19), a loaded word that may well mean his ultimate future salvation but also likely points to the present vindication of Paul and his ministry in the trial about to occur.

Altogether, this whole passage breathes confidence and *hope*, not wane wishfulness, but Paul's *hope-filled expectation that whatever happens, Christ will be magnified in him*. The key word *exalt* (v. 20) literally means to make large, here to magnify in the sense of Christ becoming even more visible and well known to people through Paul's trial, no matter the outcome—"whether by life or by death." In a final aside (vv. 21–26), Paul now reflects on his future, his own life or death, and how Jesus would be magnified in either case. In one of Paul's finest moments, he utters some of the most well-known and beloved words in the New Testament: "For to me, to live is Christ and to die is gain" (v. 21).

Looking at the two alternatives, Paul poses himself a hypothetical question: "What shall I choose?" (v. 22). While being set free or being executed was not really Paul's choice, his responses to that self-question reveal much about Paul's spiritual heart and viewpoint of hope in the face of life-or-death alternatives.

Yearning for the End ("To Die Is Gain")

AFTER DEATH THERE WILL BE NO MORE SEPARATION, BUT A DIRECT AND INTIMATELY PERSONAL EMBRACE BY THE LORD JESUS.

Paul wrestles internally with this life-or-death dilemma and finds that he is "torn between the two" (1:23). He seems uncertain or ambivalent about his choice, though if it were a matter of preference, Paul's desire was death. The key point is Paul's sincere *yearning* ("desire") for the end of his earthly life. But why does he long so for it? It is crucial that we see precisely how Paul expresses *why* he has this earnest yearning for death, which he considers obviously better: "I desire to depart and be with Christ, which is better by far" (v. 23).

Departure ("To Depart")

First of all, Paul simply says he desires "to depart." Throughout human history people have often expressed a desire for death, mainly to escape their present agonies. We see this almost universal sentiment in the movie *Gladiator,* where the main character, Maximus, lost all that was precious to him. His father-figure emperor was murdered, his honor and status stripped away, his family killed, his possessions confiscated, and he himself was enslaved. He wanted to die. Bereft of everything he held dear, all he had left was a death wish.

However, such a viewpoint of Paul's desire "to depart" would be a distortion of the spirit of Paul in this letter to the Philippians, a letter that exudes a sense of joy and fullness of life. Clearly Paul did not understand "to depart" as a disillusioned suicidal escapism—dissatisfaction with life and a desire to just be "done with it all." Yet, "depart" did mean for him a leaving, a departure from an old location. The verb for "depart" has a variety of uses, though always with a sense of leaving something behind permanently—a ship leaving a harbor, an army on the march breaking camp and moving on. Leaving behind once and for all their perishable, old bodies

DEATH, THEN, ULTIMATELY MEANS JOYFUL UNION WITH CHRIST.

with all their mortal limitations, believers in Christ, when they die, break camp in this world and move on. But however true it is that a believer, when he dies, is freed from sin, evil, pain, suffering, and broken-down bodies, Paul's eye here is fixed less on his departure than on his destination. He yearns to leave because of where he is going!

Destination ("To ... Be with Christ")

Paul yearns for the end of his life because then he will have reached the goal of his living, the certain realization of his one passion, to be "with Christ." In this sense, then, for Paul his death is "gain." With the phrase "to ... be with Christ," Paul centers on his *relationship* with Jesus. After death there will be no more separation, but a direct and intimately personal embrace by the Lord Jesus. Paul wrote to the Corinthian church similarly: "We are confident, I say, and would prefer to be away from the body and *at home with the Lord*" (2 Cor. 5:8). No wonder believers have coined the hope-filled term *homegoing* to talk about the death of fellow Christians. Through faith in Jesus, for a believer the sting of death has been removed by Jesus' death on the cross for his or her sins (1 Cor. 15:55). There will be no more separation, no place they will ever be that Jesus is not with them. Death, then, ultimately means joyful union with Christ.

> TIME DOES NOT HEAL, BUT THE TIMELESS TRUTH OF GOD'S LOVE IN CHRIST AND OF "CHRIST IN YOU, THE HOPE OF GLORY" (COL. 1:27) BRINGS HEALING AND HOPE, NOW AND FOREVER.

Will a believer be *consciously* with Christ at death? In addition to other solid evidence in the New Testament (see Luke 16:22–31), the language and strong feelings in this passage are nonsense unless there is a full consciousness of the believer in Jesus' presence. At no time will a Christian be apart from Christ— ever—though the second coming of Christ and the believers' receiving of their resurrection bodies remains yet future. Nevertheless, Paul saw death as a path that would bring him into Jesus' presence.

Not long after Rachel's death, I sat in my office just after teaching this passage in a class. Agonizing over my loss, I broke down in tears on my desk. When the professor across the hall came in to check on me, all I could do was choke out the words, "I don't want to be here anymore; I just want to die and go home." To his credit, he did not get alarmed or chastise me. He just sat and helped me cry. You see, I knew Rachel's genuine and warm faith in Christ, and knowing that she was with Christ, I found myself overwhelmed with the desire to depart and join her in Jesus' presence in heaven. I was not disillusioned, nor was I suicidal, but I simply felt that same yearning for death Paul had—seeing it as "gain" in so many ways. I could almost taste heaven's reality at that moment. Yet I knew that my life or death was not my decision to make, whatever my desire might be.

Yet Living Now for Eternity ("To Live Is Christ")

Over the years, I cannot remember how often I have heard the old adage "Time heals all things." People usually say it with a sympathetic and knowing nod of the head as if it will help me. Well, it just is not true. The mere passage of time only means more brain cells have died off, and so my memories have begun (frustratingly) to fade, but it does not bring real healing to my broken heart. Time does not heal, but the timeless truth of God's love in Christ and of "Christ in you, the hope of glory" (Col. 1:27) brings healing and hope, now and forever. But what we actually *do* with time—living in faith, true hope, and love—does have the power to heal.

Without hesitation or any sense of misgiving, having turned over in his mind the alternatives of life and death, Paul knows that he will go on living ("remain in the body," Phil. 1:24–25). What will he do with his time? Once again in the biblical text itself we see that *how he views* this life alternative brings us to the spiritual heart of Paul—a viewpoint of hope that we would all do well to follow—as he devotes himself to living now in light of eternity.

Passion-Driven Person

Paul's powerfully succinct statement, "To me, to live is Christ," shows a man on a mission. In popular parlance, we might say Paul was a "purpose-driven" person. But however true that may be, "to live is Christ" takes us more deeply into Paul's heart, penetrating past goals to the very ground of grace, his trusting love relationship with the Lord. He could only be a purposeful man of God because he was a passion-driven person. As Paul wrote to the Corinthians, "Christ's love compels us" (2 Cor. 5:14). That passionate love relationship with Christ drove Paul onward, empowering him for purposeful living. As he told his Philippian friends later in this same letter: "I consider everything a loss compared to the surpassing greatness of knowing Christ Jesus my Lord, for whose sake I have lost all things. I consider them rubbish, that I may gain Christ and be found in him" (3:8–9).

WE MUST NEVER FORGET THOSE GOD HAS GIVEN US TO CARE FOR, BECAUSE IN REMOVING OURSELVES FROM OTHERS WE REMOVE OURSELVES FROM THE COMMUNAL, GIVE-AND-TAKE, LOVING CONTEXT WHERE WE, TOO, WILL EXPERIENCE HOPE AND HEALING.

Everything comes into focus when Paul says, "For to me, to live is Christ and to die is gain." His passionate attachment to Jesus puts to shame all halfhearted, ritualistic shams of religiosity, exposing their insipid and lifeless falsity. The symphony of life for Paul is played from start to finish in the key of Christ. There is no other scale for the music of his soul. Any spiritual progress and joy we might have depend utterly upon our sharing with Paul, both individually and in communities, that same passionate, primary, and singular heart devotion to Jesus. The problem, of course, is that we often voice such passion while living quite differently.

In a self-gratification culture, we are conditioned to let work, wealth, worldly pleasures, and a welter of other concerns put Christ off to the periphery of our lives or out of the picture entirely. To make Christ anything other than the primary passion and singular center of our lives will drain God's grace and true hope from our existence. Hope is, from start to finish, all about the passionate love of God for us in Jesus, realized by our passionate embracing in faith of that love in return. For Paul, "For to me, to live is Christ" says it all—and it should do so for us as well.

Placed with People

Writing that his ongoing living is "necessary for you" (1:24) helps describe how Paul now sees his reason for being. He understands his continued living in this world means healthy and helpful personal relationships with people in the faith community. Interestingly, Paul did not just say he would "remain" but added further that he would "continue with" them (v. 25). The second phrase literally means to "remain alongside" someone, a vivid picture of ongoing intimate connection with people.

He is no Lone Ranger but knows God has placed him for now with people who need him. When experiencing hard times, such as grieving the death of a loved one, we can easily become so self-absorbed and focused on dulling the pain that we withdraw from others in an unhealthy way. Paul's words tell us that we must never forget those God has given us to care for, because in removing ourselves from others we remove ourselves from the communal, give-and-take, loving context where we, too, will experience hope and healing. Just before Jesus ascended back to heaven, leaving his disciples alone to face hard times, he asked Peter three times if he loved him. Three times Peter said, "Yes," and three times Jesus responded in turn, "Feed and take care of my sheep" (John 21:15–17). Truly, to love Christ means feeding and taking care of others, courageously continuing with them in loving relationships.

Progress and Produce

Paul anticipates "fruitful" (Phil. 1:22) results from his ongoing life's labor, namely their overflowing "progress and joy in the faith" (vv. 25–26). Paul expects that by working alongside them again he will be a catalyst for Christlike growth in their lives, producing an ever-increasing quality and quantity of the fruit of the Holy Spirit in them.

Following Rachel's death, so many of her fellow students from Gordon Russell Middle School shared about her kindness to other students, her joyful spirit, and her generous, loving Christian heart—the fruit of the Spirit—that an annual award for virtuous living was instituted in that public school: the Rachel Terveen Virtue Award. The character qualifications of virtue for the award came straight from the scriptural description of the fruit of the Spirit in Galatians 5:22–23 and the nature of love in 1 Corinthians 13:4–7. Year after year, as the students and staff work through the nominations and the decision for that year's recipient, the fruit of Rachel's life continues to touch them all, serving as a catalyst beckoning them toward true love and lasting joy—toward Christ himself. What a magnificent heritage of love to leave behind!

In our own family, Rachel's loving heart served as a catalyst for us to respond by pouring out our own hearts in new, loving directions. I think of the two babies we've adopted as "Rachel's children," and oftentimes I can almost feel her smiling over our home as we chase these two joyful bundles of energy. The heritage of hope and love passes on now, extending grace to new generations.

Where Is the Hope?

Paul grounds his hope now and forever in Christ Jesus and in his passionate, primary, and singular personal attachment to him in loving faith. Through his hope-filled, confident expectation of salvation in Jesus, now and ultimately, Paul views whatever happens in his life as resulting in progress and joy. Through suffering and hardships, bonds become bridges of God's grace! Whether living on or dying, for Paul, Christ grows greater—magnified in and through Paul himself. Such certain, Christ-centered hope may be known by all who join the voices of their hearts to Paul's passionate heart's cry of faith: *"For to me, to live is Christ and to die is gain."*

"HERE IS MY HEART, LORD ..."

Lord, like Paul, I, too, have parts of my life that feel like "chains," binding me up and holding me down. I need to just talk with you about ...

I believe that you, Jesus, can help me learn how I can turn my bonds into bridges of real gospel hope both for myself and others. Lord, help me to ...

God, sometimes I get upset, hurt, and angry at what people do and say to me because of what I am going through—dumb things that are not really helpful at all. When this happens, help me to ...

Given what has happened to me, it is hard, Lord, to even imagine any "progress and joy" in any of it. So teach me, Jesus, how to let you be magnified, seen more clearly in me, through what I am going through right now when ...

Lord God, when I think about the end of my own life, I am really down and feel like ...

... But your Word teaches me to see it with hope as "gain" and to even yearn for it because ...

Lord Jesus, I want to know for myself the reality of life that Paul experienced when he said, "For to me, to live is Christ," especially in areas of my ...

... Passionate heart attachment to you ...

... Place with people ...

... Progress in fruitful impact on others ...

Lord, bring me someone with whom I can share my renewed hope that I now see in Paul's words, "For to me, to live is Christ and to die is gain," especially how in my life ...

Chapter 12

THE FINISH LINE: LEAVING A LEGACY OF LOVE AND HOPE

—— 2 TIMOTHY 4:6–8 ——

Ahead of us all lies our own finish line. Many faithful followers of Jesus have crossed before us and left behind legacies that call us to follow in their steps. In his last letter with his final words to his "son" Timothy, Paul speaks personally about the heart of his legacy … a legacy of faith, love, and hope.

The award-winning ballad "Three Wooden Crosses," by famed country singer Randy Travis, tells the story of a farmer, a teacher, a hooker, and a preacher riding together on a bus. A terrible accident takes the lives of all but the hooker, to whom the preacher with his dying breath hands his bloodstained Bible. Through the Word of God, then, her life's course was changed. She read its truth to her son and passed that very Bible on to him. Now a gospel preacher, he tells the story and holds the Bible high "for all of us to see," a legacy and a lesson of love and grace. The farmer left his son faith and love for growing things. The teacher left wisdom in the minds of numerous children. The preacher left the love of God in the Scriptures, a love the hooker received and left in turn with her son. So, the song tells us, three wooden crosses line the right side of a highway, and now we know why there were not four. We hear the song's heart in its chorus: "It's not what you take when you leave this world behind you; *it's what you leave behind you when you go.*"

STRUGGLING FOR THE GOSPEL IS THE GRANDEST LIFE BATTLE OF ALL!

We all receive legacies by those who have died before us—some wonderful elements but also some not-so-great parts. In turn, when our time comes, we also will leave behind a legacy, and it, too, will have its grand and less-than-excellent parts. What kinds of legacies have been left for you? What kind of legacy do you want to pass down to your loved ones?

I have delivered many sermons and eulogies for funerals and written several obituaries as well, including those of loved ones. Though it sounds morbid, I once tried to write my own obituary as well—ahead of time. I found, interestingly, that it pushed me to consider more than just factual aspects of work history, hobbies, accomplishments, and family connections. It revealed the heart of my hopes and dreams, a legacy of what I truly loved in my life—what I really treasured and would most desire to leave behind me when I go.

Hunched over in a Roman prison cell and realizing his death was at hand, Paul writes his last New Testament letter—his second letter to Timothy—and addresses it to Timothy, "my dear son" (2 Tim. 1:2). He was critically concerned that his gospel legacy not be abandoned, but rather expanded. Over fifteen years earlier in Lystra, Timothy's hometown, Paul was stoned by an angry mob and left for dead after preaching the gospel (see Acts 14). However, out of the rubble some became believers, including Timothy's mother, Eunice, and grandmother Lois—who passed on the faith to young Timothy (see 2 Tim. 1:5). A short time later, Timothy joined Paul's band of brothers and never left his side, sharing all his missionary joys and adversities and becoming like a son to him. Now, nearing the end of his life and seized by a sense of urgency, Paul knows he needs to pass the baton. So he writes Timothy one last time to motivate and encourage him to carry on the gospel work they had labored on together for nearly fifteen years.

Paul draws his warm letter of encouragement to a close with a final urgent charge (4:1–5) to the youthful Timothy. "Preach the Word" (v. 2) heads a series of nine imperatives critical for Timothy's future ministry, especially now that Paul's death loomed so near. The legacy of faith, hope, and love had to live on. Paul ends his final, fervent charge to Timothy in a very personal way, pointing Timothy to his own life's legacy as inspiration and a worthy model to follow and pass on (vv. 6–8). Likewise, we also should walk in the steps of Paul and of other genuine, faithful followers of Jesus Christ who have gone before us, so that we, too, may leave behind a rich legacy of faith, hope, and love for others to follow as well. Here, then, in this passage, Paul's legacy still speaks to all believers, a legacy of true love and hope—a legacy that looks both back to the past and ahead to the future.

LOOK BACK ... AND LEARN (2 TIM. 4:6–7)

Paul abruptly changes direction in 4:6, looking away from Timothy and to himself. His time is almost over, but he wants Timothy to remember his life, learn from it, and live on wisely in light of it. Paul uses two interesting images to refer to his death. First, like a "drink offering" (of wine) poured out completely at the foot of the sacrificial altar (Num. 28:7), Paul's lifeblood was even now being emptied to the very last drop in sacrificial obedience to the Lord. Paul then shifts his death imagery to that of a ship departing a port, "loosed" (literally) from its moorings. Like a ship whose departure time approached, he, too, would be leaving these earthly shores.[1] Together these images picture his death not only as an ending and a leaving but also as a release to embark on a new joyous journey … "to depart and be with Christ" (Phil. 1:23). But before he goes, Paul wants us to look back and learn from his life's legacy how we, too, can live a life joyfully poured out to the last drop in loving devotion to the Lord.

With three perfectly balanced parallel phrases in 4:7 and using some of his favorite military and athletic imagery for following Jesus, Paul reminds Timothy and us all that he fought hard, finished well, and followed faithfully. The original language especially emphasizes the three verbs, each pointing to a past action of Paul that has resulted in Paul's now being who he is. He fought hard and stands now as a *fighter*. He ran to the end of the race and stands now as a *finisher*. He kept on faithfully following Jesus and stands now as a *faithful follower*. Fighter, finisher, and faithful follower—what a grand legacy to live by and pass on to others!

Fight Hard

Paul first concisely and simply says, "I have fought the good fight." The term "fight" was used then (just like today) for either military or athletic imagery, but in either case the keynote is the same—*struggle*. The word itself gives us our English word *agony*, which implies intensely energetic exertion, a "battle" waged against difficult opposition and a "battle" that includes willingly enduring suffering. Throughout Paul's life as a Christian, he *struggled* for the gospel, giving it everything he had, fighting hard when opposed and enduring suffering when necessary. Paul fought hard; he knew no other way. This struggle left no place for lackadaisical, flabby, halfhearted effort but demanded his all. He lived his Christian life for all it was worth. He could do no less.

In a recent Olympic wrestling competition, a legendary Russian wrestler walked with a confident swagger to the mat. None gave his opponent, the young American from Wyoming, Rulon Gardner, any chance against the undefeated Russian. The athletic world reeled with shock when Gardner won the match and wrapped himself in his nation's flag, exulting in triumph. Some time later, at the end of Gardner's final wrestling match as an amateur, he sat down and, after untying the laces of his wrestling shoes, laid them solemnly in the center of the wrestling mat—a symbol of the end of his Olympic career and that he had given his all. In a similar way last year, an excellent college basketball player at Providence University ended his four-year college career with the same gesture. He unlaced his basketball shoes and left them in the middle of the floor, a poignant symbol that he had "left it all on the court" for his team. What a picture to imagine the apostle Paul, having packed up his pen and papyrus, unlacing his sandals that had traveled so many miles on missionary journeys on Roman roads and then laying them down … on the cold floor of a Roman jail cell.

GOD ALONE IN HIS WISDOM KNOWS THE KIND OF TERRAIN EACH OF US TRAVELS, AND HE ALONE KNOWS WHERE OUR FINISH LINE IS.

Over the years, I have had many heart-to-heart talks with friends, family, and colleagues who have battled various kinds of cancer. Time and again the words *fight* and *struggle* come up to describe their experience battling against this dire disease enemy. Though the prognosis all too often appears bleak and the surgeries, X-rays, and chemotherapy treatments are brutally hard on their weakened bodies, I have watched with admiration as they bravely fight for their lives. It takes all they have, but as they look through the pain at those they love, they know it is a fight worth fighting.

Though the price of believing in Jesus will cost Paul his life, he does not regret the fight. In fact, he calls it a "good" fight. Struggling for the gospel is the grandest life battle of all. It is worthwhile because it is for God and his good news in Christ. It is worthwhile because only the gospel fight can bring real hope, life, and love to hopeless, dying, and lonely people. Above all, it is worthwhile because Jesus, too, entered this human arena of life and suffering and fought the "good fight" for God's own love for sinners to the very end. His struggle concluded as he unlaced the heartstrings of his life and laid it down … on a cross.

Finish Well

At the close of his third missionary journey, Paul spoke his final time with the leaders of the church in Ephesus. Knowing that suffering and prison lay ahead of him and knowing also that he would never see these loved ones again, he passionately shared his heart: "I consider my life worth nothing to me, if only I may *finish the race* and complete the task the Lord Jesus has given me—the task of testifying to the gospel of God's grace" (Acts 20:24). Now, five years later and having suffered in three different prisons during that time, Paul had completed the task and uses the same language in retrospect to tell Timothy, "I have *finished the race.*"

Paul loved athletic imagery, often the idea of a race. This passage makes me think especially of a relay kind of race in which each of us has his own shorter leg of the longer course to run as part of a team. In our area, one of the biggest races is the Hood-to-Coast run. Numerous teams join this race, beginning high on Mount Hood and ending on the sands of the Pacific Ocean. Some runners (and teams) run swiftly, but other runners (and teams) go slowly. Some run downhill legs, while others have uphill pulls. Some run on smooth pavement, and others trudge through heavy sand. Some run longer stretches; others run shorter portions. But all run (or walk), and every team rejoices when its last team member crosses the finish line and all the team members join together, splashing in the sea. Though they do give awards for finishing order, the far greater measure of success in this race is completing the journey to the sea … finishing the race.

Paul *finished* his part of the race. He does not puff out his chest pridefully. He's satisfied to have endured to the end. He is content to have finished his leg of the great gospel race, to have done his part and now hand off the baton of ministry to Timothy to continue with the next leg. He was a *finisher*. Paul persevered to the end in the part of the race God had assigned him to run. Notably, we find the very same word—"finish"—on Jesus' lips while on the cross. Having given his entire life, having loved us to the end, and having taken on himself the deadly cost of our sinfulness, Jesus said, "It is finished" (John 19:30). Jesus was "tempted in every way, just as we are" (Heb. 4:15), even tempted to quit and give up on the task the Father God had given him. But in perfect love Jesus endured to the very end, the ultimate finisher.

WHATEVER LENGTH OUR LIFE'S COURSE MAY BE OR HOWEVER CHALLENGING THE TERRAIN, EACH OF US IS CALLED BY GOD'S GRACE TO FINISH THE RACE OF FAITH, HOPE, AND LOVE SET BEFORE US.

We all have our legs of the race to run … and to finish. God alone in his wisdom knows the kind of terrain each of us travels, and he alone knows where our finish line is. There is much we do not understand. Some, like Rachel, come to their own finish lines far too soon for us and are gone. They burn brightly, though all too briefly. Others, like my father, live on into old age with only a flicker of light at the end. Yet, whatever length our life's course may be or however challenging the terrain, each of us is called by God's grace to finish the race of faith, hope, and love set before us.

Follow Faithfully

Paul closes his threefold look at his past simply by saying, "I have kept the faith." Though we may find ourselves pushed to the limit by grievous sufferings and losses, assaulted by doubts about God's goodness and truth, and tempted even to compromise or abandon our faith in God in the face of a hostile culture, Paul's words here summon us to "[keep] the faith," to follow faithfully.

This phrase was commonplace in antiquity for firm faithfulness to a trust, a *persevering loyalty*. In this athletic context, Paul's phrase here may suggest the ancient athlete's sworn oath to abide fully by the rules for participating in the games. Paul valued loyalty, a personal fidelity most clearly authenticated when demonstrated in the midst of great trial. The apostle would have appreciated the motto of the United States Marine Corps, *Semper Fidelis* ("always faithful"), emphasizing their legendary fierce loyalty to one another in the heat of battle. Though Paul himself would be deserted by friends (Demas and others, 2 Tim. 4:10, 16–18; 1:15), and enemies would do all they could to hurt him (Alexander, 4:14–15), Paul stayed loyal to his ministry and to his Lord, who "stood at my side and gave me strength" (4:17). He *followed faithfully*.

Grieving the loss of a loved one is a trial that places severe stress on relationships. Many marriages and families break apart on the rocky shoals of the trials of deep grief, and relationships with God also hit rough waters. Timothy's relationship with the believers in Ephesus was difficult and posed many challenges, so Paul wanted to encourage him to follow his example and persevere in that relationship. Through whatever may come our way, Paul wants us to know that Jesus will always stand by our side and grant us sufficient grace to persevere in the relationships he has given us. In doing this, we also keep faith with the one—Jesus—who so perfectly keeps faith with us.

With the phrase "[keep] the faith," Paul also means we must *preserve the truth* of the gospel message—keep *the faith* intact and uncorrupted by false teaching. In Timothy's time many people preferred teachers to tell them what they wanted to hear (4:3–4) and so turned aside from the gospel truth to alluring "myths" and stories. Little has changed in our time, and people still too easily accept foolish theories (such as the so-called Da Vinci Code phenomenon) and purely humanistic answers to our concerns and problems. When I left for Edinburgh, Scotland, to pursue doctoral studies there, my dear, wise old uncle Ed took me aside and warned me soberly not to "lose my faith" in that liberal environment. Pressures to turn away may come from many angles, internal and external, so we need to heed Paul's warning to hold firmly to the pattern of sound words found in the Bible, to guard the gospel treasure entrusted to us (2 Tim. 1:13–14) ... to keep "the faith."

LOOK AHEAD ... WITH LONGING
(2 TIM. 4:8)

Just before his final farewells, with his last words here (4:8), Paul looks ahead to the future, and that, too, is a part of his legacy. Paul wants Timothy and us to be people who, like himself, look ahead with longing. This was not something new for Paul that he was doing now near the end of his life. As a believer, he had always looked at his life through the lenses of eternity, living in light of the sure hope of heaven. His confidence that his faith in Christ would be rewarded colored every part of his existence. He longed for the day he would receive the crown of righteousness stored up for him.

Confidence That Justice Will Be Done

Paul would soon appear in the court of the prejudiced and perverted Nero, but Paul knew his puny judgment meant nothing in light of the perfect justice to be rendered by the "righteous Judge," Jesus (4:1, 8), when he calls his supreme court to order at his second "appearing." Paul knows that Judge Jesus is "righteous," totally qualified to pass perfectly just verdicts and carry out those judgments. Paul finds assurance and comfort in that thought. Nero might pass a death sentence on Paul, but one day Jesus would reverse that decision and give Paul an "eternal life sentence" instead!

In a world filled with injustice and evil that all too often go unpunished, we long for the day when justice will be done and things will finally be made right. Paul knew that God demonstrated his justice already, when on the cross Jesus—the one truly righteous man the world would ever see—paid the death penalty with his own blood for the sins of all who believe in him (Rom. 3:23–26). Isaiah prophesied, "There is no God apart from me, a righteous God and a Savior; there is none but me. Turn to me and be saved, all you ends of the earth.... Before me every knee will bow; by me every tongue will swear. They will say of me, 'In the LORD alone are righteousness and strength'" (Isa. 45:21–24). In the Lord Jesus alone is hope of forgiveness of our sins, a hope of righteousness realized solely in those who trust only and wholly in Jesus as their Savior. Paul knew with complete confidence that God's righteous justice in Christ would, in the future on "that day" of judgment, come to its final complete and

AT HIS RETURN, THE PAIN OF SEPARATION FROM JESUS HIMSELF AND BELIEVING LOVED ONES WILL END.

perfect expression—an eternal life "sentence" for those who have by faith put their lives in Jesus' hands, but a death sentence for all who are not in Christ. Though God yet patiently waits for people to turn to him, one day that door of opportunity will close … and justice will be done.

Crown of Righteousness That Will Be Awarded

Picking up athletic imagery once again, Paul refers to the "crown" (or better, "wreath") awarded to the victors at the finish line (see also 2:5 and 1 Cor. 9:25). However, instead of a green-leafed crown, Paul anticipates receiving quite a different kind of glorious crown on judgment day.

At Jesus' second coming in glory—his "appearing"—Jesus, the *righteous* life-race Judge, fittingly awards a "crown *of righteousness*." What, however, is such a crown?[2] Paul knew that, though Christians already receive "righteousness" through Jesus and are—at the moment of faith— adopted as children into God's own family, that personal, intimate relationship with the Lord is not yet fully and finally experienced in this broken world. Even though we are born again as his children, we still sin and we still physically die. Clearly a final stage of righteousness yet remains. Yet future then, the "crown *of righteousness*" must refer to the full realization of a direct and unimpeded relationship with God, even becoming equipped with resurrection bodies (1 Cor. 15) perfectly suited for such an unrestricted restored relationship with the Lord in his heavenly home.

Paul quickly adds that such a "crown of righteousness" awaits not just him—as if he is some sort of special case—but "all who have longed for his appearing." The phrase "longed for" translates literally "loved." The verbal tense points to the constant and unchanging character of the lives of true followers of Jesus—they *love* (hence "long for") the very thought of Jesus' second coming. It is no accident that Paul, just two verses later when sadly talking about Demas who deserted him (2 Tim. 4:10), simply says he "loved this world"—a stark contrast to a true lover of God. Love for Jesus' return marks every true Christian.

Assured of relationship with the Lord only getting yet greater, a believer boldly (1 John 2:28) looks forward to Jesus' appearing again. Having loved Jesus by faith in his first coming, a true believer also loves the very thought of that faith being fulfilled totally—receiving the "crown of righteousness"—and seeing Jesus face-to-face at his second coming!

I cannot remember a time as a Christian when I did not look forward to Jesus' second coming, whether I understood it fully or not. But when Rachel died at only fourteen, and I was yet in my forties, Jesus' return became much more than just good doctrine. It meant life, love, and hope for me. I discovered within myself a deep and passionate yearning for Jesus' appearing as never before. Now, I love the very thought of the "blessed hope" (Titus 2:13) of Jesus' soon return, for I know that at his return, the pain of separation from Jesus himself and believing loved ones will end. We will all be together and embrace one another again. To this day, sermons, songs, and Scriptures that speak of Jesus' return touch me deeply, often bringing tears of longing and anticipation. Not by coincidence, probably the oldest Christian prayer preserved in the New Testament is the Aramaic word "*Maranatha*" (1 Cor. 16:22), a cry that means "Our Lord, come!" Nor is it a coincidence that at the close of the Bible in Revelation 22:20, "Come, Lord Jesus" reflects this same heartfelt plea for Jesus to return. As this passionate longing for his appearing marked the earliest believers, it has continued to mark all true believers ever since. May the hope of this prayer etch itself deeply into all our souls, a hope for the heartbroken throughout the ages.

Where Is the Hope?

The apostle Paul left a rich legacy of faith, love, and hope that has extended to two thousand years of believers, modeling a message of encouragement to carry on courageously in living for Christ in the midst of great trials. We find our hope renewed by looking at Paul—who fought with all he had, finished the course set before him, and followed the way of Jesus faithfully. With Jesus at our side, we, too, can run.

Having joined a stadium full of a "great cloud of witnesses" (Heb. 12:1), Paul and the ranks of runners who have finished their gospel race ahead of us call us to take heart and "run with perseverance the race marked out for us." Finally, we find hope as well when, with Paul, we look ahead with passionate longing to Jesus' return. On "that day" in the company of believers throughout the ages, our relationship with Jesus will be fully and finally fulfilled—as we are awarded the "crown of righteousness." So with the ancient prayer of believers, we, too, cry out in faith, love, and hope, "Maranatha, come, Lord Jesus!"

"HERE IS MY HEART, LORD ..."

Lord, when I think of my loved one(s) who have died, I remember what they have left as a legacy for me. Not all are perfect memories, but I do cherish especially ...

... And to honor their memory, help me to ...

I'm concerned, Jesus, that my life's legacy for my own loved ones is not all that it should be.

I confess that I've messed up when ...

Help me to begin building a better legacy now by ...

Oh God, like Timothy, when I experience hard trials in life, I find myself tempted to just stop trying and give up.

I admit that what I am going through makes me feel ...

I need your strength and encouragement to fight and finish,
so please help me to …

Dear Lord, in the face of suffering, sometimes questions about you
and your ways trouble me and make it hard to keep the faith. When
this happens, help me remember that …

I admit, God, that the injustices in this broken world really upset me.
Help me remember, Lord, that you are a "righteous Judge"
and that one day …

When I think of your second coming, Jesus, I passionately long for it,
especially because it means …

Lord, help me today to begin building anew a legacy of faith, love, and
hope in the lives of those you have given to me, especially …

READERS' GUIDE

For Personal Reflection or
Group Discussion

READERS' GUIDE

Hope can actually seem like a bad word sometimes. When placed in front of someone who is grieving the loss of a loved one, it may seem trite, simplistic, and unhelpful. But hope is indeed real. It is more than just a word. It is a healing truth. And it comes from the very One who best understands loss and the pain that it brings.

If you're grieving, you already know the constant longing for hope. The questions that follow will help you on your journey to discover true hope. Take the time to read each chapter of the book; then read and reflect on the questions in this guide. While these are helpful to work through on your own, you might find additional value in working on them with a close friend or family member, or perhaps even in a small group. Keep in mind that these questions sometimes go to very deep, personal places in your soul. If you're uncomfortable answering some of them now, don't feel bad about that. Though the components of grieving are similar for everyone, the timing and manifestation of these components are different for each person.

Spend time in prayer before you approach these questions—ask God to open your heart and mind to the truth that you know and the truth that he offers. Then spend additional time in prayer after you've examined the questions, asking God to continue providing you with hope and the healing hope can provide.

Don't be afraid to let your emotions flow honestly out of this reflection. There are no right answers to these questions—except those that are true for you. God wants to meet you just where you are in this time—take the time to discover where that is.

And then trust God's Holy Spirit to guide you through the desert. Along the way, God's Word will provide you with an oasis of hope just when you need it.

PART ONE: VISIONS OF HOPE

CHAPTER 1
WILL FAITH SURVIVE?

1. If you have suffered a "crisis of faith" after a loss, how did that manifest itself? What, if anything, changed in your approach to church?

2. The question "Why do good people suffer and bad people seem to prosper?" has been asked by many hurting people. Have you asked this question? If so, how have you dealt with those feelings? How easy is it for you to come to the conclusion that "God is good" in light of your feelings?

3. Think about "embittered envy." How have you experienced this? In what ways have you known "frustrated anger"?

4. The author states: "[Asaph's] doubts do not lead to unbelief. Only real faith could be troubled by such things." What is your initial reaction to this statement? What does this suggest is true about "real faith"?

5. Entering the "sanctuary of God" is a critical step in the journey to hope. If you have done this, what was it like to take that step? If you haven't, what is holding you back?

6. Think about the things that make you wonder about God's goodness. How can you move from doubt to trust in these areas of your life? How might you begin to recognize the sufficiency of Christ in these circumstances?

CHAPTER 2
A DEATH MOST PRECIOUS

1. As you consider the valleys or lows of your life, what picture of God comes to mind? Is he near? Distant? Uncaring? Asking you to be patient? What does it mean to be suffering "in the context of a testimony of faith"?

2. If you have honestly expressed your heart's feelings about your losses, how has that affected your relationship with God? In what ways does expressing your feelings open up the path for hope?

3. Share your reaction to the following statement: "God keeps on listening to us and knows far more of our situation than we imagine." How does that make you feel? What truths do you hear in this statement?

4. Psalm 116:15 says that God's children are precious. In what ways have you felt that preciousness in the midst of pain? In what ways have you not felt that way?

5. Is it easy to think of who you are before the Lord when life all around is so painful? Why or why not? What little steps can you take toward the goal of "walking before the Lord"?

6. How does it make you feel to know that God grieves with you? In what palpable ways does this offer hope?

CHAPTER 3
SORROWS UNENDING, HOPE UNDYING

1. Make a list of defining moments in your life. How many of these are sorrowful or painful moments? What feelings shoot to the surface as you recall these moments?

2. In what ways can you relate to Jeremiah's Lamentations? How
    are these passionate expressions of pain like your own expres-
    sions of pain?

3. Do you naturally hide your strong feelings or express them? If
    you tend to hide or repress them, how might Lamentations
    speak to that? What is it like for you to "pour out your heart
    like water to God"?

4. What are some of the "bright threads" that are woven into your
    story? What are the challenges of waiting on the Lord when you
    are grieving?

5. Read Lamentations 3:22–24. How does God's "great love" reach
    out to you in your pain? What might it take for you to embrace
    the truth of that love?

6. There is hope in the final poem in Lamentations—hope
    couched in Jeremiah's pleas. What pleas would you like to
    speak or cry out to God? Speak or write them honestly and
    from a place of hopefulness.

CHAPTER 4
VOICES OF COMFORT IN THE DESERT

1. How have you felt the "sense of exile" that was at the core of the story for the Jewish nation? In what ways is it comforting to know that your tears are not the first, nor the last, to come from the pain of loss?

2. What are the voices of comfort you've heard in the middle of crisis? How can God's Word be a voice of comfort for you? Have you ever felt like someone was "throwing Scripture" at you in an effort to help? How did you react to that?

3. Are there things you need to clear away before you can receive God's comfort? What might those be? How will you go about clearing them?

4. Think about your journey thus far. How is it like traveling through a desert? Do you believe it's necessary to travel through a desert on the road to recovery?

5. Respond to this statement: "Accepting the frailty and futility of our own speech and our own strength is the necessary starting point for experiencing comfort."

6. God's sovereignty is described in many ways in Isaiah 40. Which of these descriptions captures your hurting heart the most? How can these truths about God's power help you feel comforted?

PART TWO: GOSPEL OF HOPE

CHAPTER 5
IN DEEPEST WATER AND DARKEST NIGHT

1. Think about the darkest time of your perfect storm. In what ways did you feel like rescue simply wasn't going to happen? How does getting to know the person of Jesus Christ help you see that rescue is indeed a possibility?

2. What are your thoughts about the "walking on water" story? What impact does it have on you when you see it as—at least in part—a revelation of God as a God who brings hope when we feel like we're sinking in life?

3. It seems significant that Jesus comes to the disciples after they've been struggling. Does this give you hope for your story? What are your reactions to this decision by Jesus?

4. How does Jesus' announcement, "I am he," offer you encouragement?

5. Which part of Peter's role in this story can you relate to most—the boldness of getting out onto the water to walk toward Jesus or the distraction that leads to his sinking? How might Jesus be reaching his hand out to you in your story?

6. In what ways has it been difficult to worship or even acknowledge God's magnificence in the midst of your story? How easy is it to live in the paradox of trusting God for who he is and asking him to be what you need in this time?

CHAPTER 6
WHEN THERE IS NO SIGN OF LIFE

1. Consider this statement: "When there is no sign of life, God graciously provides one for us in Jesus Christ." How does this truth intersect with your story?

2. What delays and detours do you seem to be facing in life? How do these delays and detours affect the way in which you see Jesus? Does your faith feel threatened in these times? Why?

3. Much of the healing story is about trust. How do you go about trusting God when he seems absent or when you're presented with delays and detours? What role can family and friends play in helping you to trust God?

4. The promise of everlasting life is an ultimate truth that can offer some hope. Does this give you peace or hope in your story? How can you begin to see Jesus as the source of truest hope?

5. Those two words "Jesus wept" seem to carry a lot of weight. How can these words offer you comfort? How does knowing that Jesus is "not aloof from our loss, our pain" help you understand God's role in your healing?

6. How does God's sign of life manifest itself in your story? What comfort can you find in the truth that you can still believe in Jesus even when life takes away someone you love?

Chapter 7
In the Face of Death

1. What are the first thoughts that come to mind when you think of the last moments spent with a loved one before his or her death? How might these thoughts be similar to the thoughts the disciples had after Jesus was crucified?

2. Do you have godly friends you can seek out for comfort? If so, how can you reach out to them? If not, what do you need to do to find some?

3. Have you experienced the "dangerous time of spiritual warfare" after the loss of a loved one? What was that like? (Or what is it like?) How can friends help when your faith is tested?

4. Is it easy or difficult for you to share your heart openly and honestly with God? How does it help you to know that Jesus expressed his heart in a vivid, deeply honest way in his greatest time of need?

5. What are your thoughts about this statement: "There is no more profound hope than in having an intimate, loving relationship with the Lord and knowing him as 'Abba, Father'"?

6. Think of ways you can go forward through grief. Which of these are you already doing? What would it take to find more ways to press forward? What does it look like to root your hope in your relationship with God?

CHAPTER 8
AFTER THE DISASTER … OPENING YOUR EYES AGAIN

1. Can you relate to the author's "migraine heartache"? In what ways have you experienced the spiritual blindness he writes about?

2. What comfort can you find in the story of Jesus' appearance on the Emmaus road? How can the truth of his grace in listening help you as you struggle with your pain?

3. Jesus leads the heartbroken disciples to the truth of his story by pointing them back to Scripture. Think of key Scriptures that have encouraged and helped you in life. How can returning to those help you through this season of loss?

4. Take a moment to "listen to your heart." What are you hearing? What might God be saying to you in this time?

5. If you are tied to a group of believers who can stand together with you, think of ways they are doing this—or ways they can help. If not, what can you do to find this kind of healing fellowship?

6. Spend a few moments reflecting on this statement: "Hope is alive because Jesus is alive." How do these words offer you comfort?

PART THREE: LETTERS OF HOPE

CHAPTER 9
GRIEVING AS THOSE WHO HAVE HOPE

1. What do you wrestle with concerning the afterlife? Do you find yourself at peace or afraid as you consider the life that follows this one on earth? Are you more hopeful or uncertain?

2. If you have lost a loved one who knew Jesus, what hope can you find in the truth of Jesus' own resurrection? How can that hope sustain you in this time?

3. The hope of a "family reunion" when Jesus returns is a powerful tool for healing. As you think of this time, what feelings come to the surface? How can these feelings build up your hope?

4. What are the greatest challenges for you in getting on with living in a way that is proper and pleasing to God? How might you go about responding to those challenges?

5. How does the encouragement of Jesus' second coming offer you hope or comfort?

6. Though Jesus promises he is "coming soon," the timetable for his return is not known to us. It may feel to you as if "soon" can't be soon enough. What are some practical ways you can keep the hope of Jesus' return alive while still going about the daily life God has given you?

Chapter 10
In the Twinkling of an Eye

1. One of the most difficult things to deal with after the loss of a loved one is the specific loss of the physical presence of that person. What hope can you find in the promise that we will all be raised with resurrection bodies after Jesus' return?

2. The certainty of Jesus' resurrection is a key teaching in Scripture. Do you wrestle with that certainty? If so, what can you do to seek trust in that teaching? If not, how can that certainty offer you hope?

3. Respond to the following statement: "Christ's resurrection cannot be disconnected in any way from a believer's own future bodily resurrection."

4. If it is true that our future bodily resurrection must impact the way we conduct ourselves in this world, what implications does that have for your own life choices in this season of grief? In the seasons of life that follow the grieving process?

5. What gives you the most hope as you consider the life after life when you and your loved ones who know Christ are given resurrection bodies?

6. Imagine what it will be like for you to be "free at last" in heaven. How can you apply that picture to the life of your loved one? In what ways can those pictures sustain you?

CHAPTER 11
HOPE: A MATTER OF LIFE OR DEATH

1. How can you turn "bonds into bridges" and let Christ be magnified in you? What about Paul's story can be an inspiration for you?

2. Do you find it easy or difficult to look at your hard times as "progress"? In what ways can you see this as a time of moving forward? What makes it difficult to see that? What are the "chains" that hold you back from progress?

3. What does it mean for you to make the main thing … the main thing? Are you doing that now? If not, what would it take to move toward that end?

4. What does "hope-filled expectation" look like to you today? What comfort can you find in the truth that God will be magnified no matter what happens?

5. How does the following statement make you feel: "Time does not heal, but the timeless truth of God's love in Christ and of 'Christ in you, the hope of glory' (Col. 1:27) brings healing and hope, now and forever"?

6. Consider where God has put you in this story. How might he be placing you among people who need you? What would it look like for you to reach out to those people?

CHAPTER 12
THE FINISH LINE: LEAVING A LEGACY OF LOVE AND HOPE

1. Think about legacies that others have left for you. Which legacies had the most positive impact on you? What do you wish your legacy would say to those who follow?

2. How does the truth that "struggling for the gospel is the grandest life battle of all" intersect with your story?

3. Is it a comfort to know that God alone knows the "terrain" you travel? If so, how is that also a hope? If not, how might it be transformed into a comfort?

4. In what ways have you felt the stress in relationships because of your grieving? What would it take to persevere in those relationships right now?

5. Does the theme of injustice have a place in your story? If so, how does the promise of God's justice help you move toward hope?

6. What legacy has your loved one left for you? Consider the memories you want to cherish, and think about them. Then ask God to build in you a hope that moves you through the grieving process with grace.

NOTES

CHAPTER 1

1. C. S. Lewis, *A Grief Observed* (New York: Bantam, 1976; from Seabury edition of 1963), 35.
2. C. S. Lewis, *The Weight of Glory* (New York: HarperCollins, 2001), 41.
3. Ibid., 42.
4. Ibid.

CHAPTER 3

1. Historically, Jeremiah conveyed in these poems part of the answer to these hard questions. God was judging them for their disobedience, a legitimate—albeit extreme—punishment for their faithlessness. While serious self-examination is called for in times of loss, as was the case with Israel, not every loss should be or can be directly connected to God's judgment. Job, for example, was guilty of no particularly sinful life to have experienced the kind of extreme suffering he did, though he did take spiritual inventory. By reasonable extension the emotional and faith heart of Lamentations can and does speak to all kinds of loss without necessarily always implying the need to lay blame or find guilt. It is also perhaps worthy of note that the writer of these laments was not personally guilty of the

nation's sins. He lays particular blame at the foot of the Jewish leadership (Lam. 4:13). He represents the voice of personal hope and faith despite the disaster unfolding all around him. Therefore, if hope exists for such a bad judgment situation, as in the case of Israel, how much more reason for hope and faith when suffering and loss are not clearly or directly connected to divine judgment. It is reasonable to extend the essential message of Lamentations to all people experiencing the various types of grief and loss.

2. H. L. Ginsberg, *The Five Megilloth and Jonah*, 2nd rev. ed. (Philadelphia: The Jewish Publication Society of America, 1969), 34.

3. Ibid., 47.

CHAPTER 8

1. John Wesley, *The Works of John Wesley, Vol.1* (London: Wesleyan Methodist Book Room, 1872), 103.

CHAPTER 11

1. Alexander Solzhenitsyn, *One Day in the Life of Ivan Denisovich*, translated by Ralph Parker (New York: New American Library, Signet, 1963), 51.

CHAPTER 12

1. Paul uses the same pair of metaphors—departure and drink offering—in Philippians (1:23; 2:17), a prison epistle of Paul's written a couple of years earlier during his first Roman imprisonment. Notably in Philippians, though he contemplates the possibility of his death there also, Paul takes a far more optimistic view for the result of the trial awaiting him at that time, expecting release and further ministry. In 2 Timothy, likely written during an unrecorded second Roman imprisonment during the time of Nero's later overt persecution of Christians, Paul now views his death as certain and already begun in a sense.

2. Interestingly, the New Testament writers use the "crown" imagery elsewhere (see 1 Cor. 9:25; 1 Thess. 2:19; James 1:12; 1 Peter 5:4; Rev. 2:10), usually with an aspect of judgment and Jesus' second coming in the context.

ABOUT THE AUTHOR

John Luke Terveen is professor of Greek and New Testament at Multnomah Biblical Seminary (Portland, Oregon; www.mult-nomah.edu), where he has taught for fifteen years. He pastored churches in South Dakota and Oregon for ten years and served three years as warden for the Edinburgh Medical Missionary Society's hostel in Scotland. His undergraduate degree was from the University of South Dakota, his graduate degree from North American Baptist Seminary, and his PhD from the University of Edinburgh. He has been married for thirty years to Laura, has a twenty-six-year-old son, Matthew; a six-year-old daughter, Anna Li; and a four-year-old daughter, Olivia Lin. His fourteen-year-old daughter, Rachel, died and went home to be with Christ in 1999. He brings a passionate love for Scripture to the tasks of teaching Greek language and New Testament exegesis. His joyful commitment to helping develop excellence in the pastoral work of biblical teaching and preaching remains central to his ongoing work in ministry contexts.

Contact Information: You may e-mail John at jterveen@mult-nomah.edu or write to him at Multnomah Biblical Seminary, 8435 NE Glisan Street, Portland, OR 97220.

Hope, and Understanding

When You Lose Someone You Love
Richard Exley

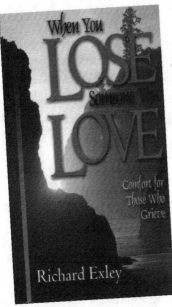

ISBN-10: 1-58919-961-8
ISBN-13: 9781589199613

*W*hen someone we love dies, we are often overwhelmed by strong emotions and confusion. Sometimes we hardly recognize ourselves or the world we live in. The process of grieving is mysterious and usually misunderstood. During this difficult and delicate time, this personal and compassionate book will touch your life with the mercy and grace of your heavenly Father. You can experience the healing warmth of God's presence and the joy of eternal life even *When You Lose Someone You Love*.

LIFE JOURNEY

To order, visit www.CookMinistries.com, or visit your favorite

Encouragement
in your time of loss

It Hurts to Lose a Special Person
Amy Ross Mumford

When death takes a "special person," it hurts. But it hurts a little less with time. And still less with more time. One morning you will wake up and your loss will not be the first thing you think about. And then you will know that it's just a bit better than it was in the beginning.

It Hurts to Lose a Special Person

Grieving the death of one you love

ISBN-10: 0-89636-093-8
ISBN-13: 9780896360938

call 1-800-323-7543
local bookstore.

COOK
COMMUNICATIONS
MINISTRIES

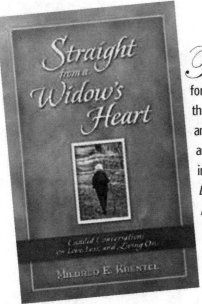

Additional copies of *HOPE FOR THE BROKENHEARTED*
and other Victor titles
are available wherever good books are sold.

If you have enjoyed this book,
or if it has had an impact on your life,
we would like to hear from you.

Please contact us at:

VICTOR BOOKS
Cook Communications Ministries, Dept. 201
4050 Lee Vance View
Colorado Springs, CO 80918

Or visit our Web site:
www.cookministries.com

The Bible Teacher's Teacher